ASIA:

A

CHRISTIAN

PERSPECTIVE

ASIA:

A CHRISTIAN PERSPECTIVE

Mary Ann Lind

Frontline Communications ● A Division of
Youth With A Mission
P.O. Box 55787
Seattle, Washington 98155

Contents

ACKNOWLEDGMENTS

No book is entirely an author's own project and certainly that is true of this book. I was especially fortunate in having the support, encouragement, and prayers of many people. To them I am deeply grateful. I wish to particularly thank Tom Bragg for guiding this book through its publication process and my editor, Beverly Haley, for her invaluable expertise. I am also grateful to Renee Taft for her expertise in typsetting this book. A special thank you goes to Loren Cunningham for his inspiration and leadership and to Dr. Howard Malmstadt, Dr. LaPrelle Martin, and Prof. Robert Lind for their contributions and suggestions. I also wish to acknowledge the assistance of Ellen and Kelly Cupples and Wilma Childers.

My appreciation also goes to Ross Tooley for material used in Chapter Eight and to Rev. Noel and Phyl Gibson for their contribution to Chapter Nine.

Finally, I gratefully acknowledge the kindness of Homer and Stephanie Noble who helped make the writing of this book possible.

To my dear mother,
with deepest gratitude

FOREWORD

Understanding God is the first priority of every person in the world. Secondly, we must understand one another. Both of these must be understood in the light of the Bible, God's Word. The Word of God is the standard by which all cultures must be measured. Every culture, including mine and yours, has within it that which is against God and against His Word. Every culture, including mine and yours, has something that is right, and we must learn to differentiate.

Dr. Mary Ann Lind has written a book on Asia in the light of the Word of God. Everyone who prays for Asia, who works or plans to work for God in Asia, conducts business in Asia, or works with Asians in their own country should read this book. I have read it. It is powerful. It is practical. And it's easy, interesting reading. You'll love it. I did.

Loren Cunningham
President, Youth With A Mission

Asia

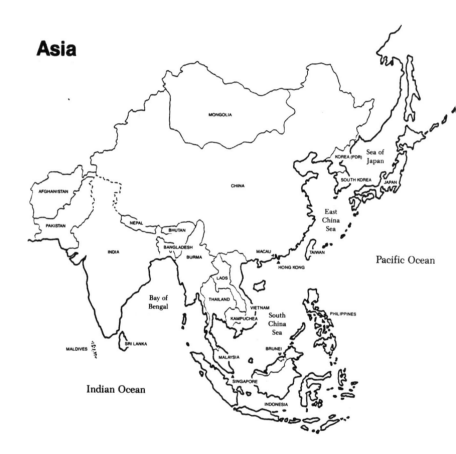

Introduction

S py out the land. That was the marching order given by Moses to his twelve spies in Numbers 13: 17-20. The Israelites were about to enter the promised land, their spiritual inheritance, and they needed to know what manner of land it was in order to assess the task which faced them.

In a similar sense, spying out the land is the purpose of this book. As Christians from every nation lay spiritual claim to lands throughout the world in fulfillment of the Great Commission (Matt. 28: 18-20), information-gathering can spell the difference between success and failure of that mission. To be more effective, we must be informed, whether we are involved directly in mission strategy, called to intercession, or simply want to expand our awareness of the world.

Specifically, this is a book about Asia, that massive area of God's creation that is home to almost two-thirds of the world's people. Not only does Asia consume a large portion of the map, but is an awakening giant whose economic heartbeat and dynamic energy combine as forces to be reckoned with worldwide.

However, the difference between this book and numerous others about Asia, is that this one presents a Christian perspective of Asia. A Christian perspective views Asia as an integrative whole in which circumstances of the past, present, and future take on a specific and comprehensive meaning because of a divine blueprint arranged by an omniscient Creator.

Such a perspective looks to the Bible for explanations and for compassionate responses to today's challenges. As Christians, we can view challenges and problems with the optimistic belief that changes for the better can occur. When God's redemptive power is at work, a change takes place in human hearts, and a change of human hearts can bring about systemic change within societies. From a Christian perspective we see opportunity and potential which can both encourage and excite us to positive action.

For example, when we view Asia from a Christian perspective, we see its geography as a magnificent showpiece of the great Creator's handiwork. But we also see the characteristics of isolation and fragmentation as a challenge to be overcome in spreading the Gospel. When we review the history of Asia, we see God's redemptive plan unfolding in ways that encourage us to believe that today's headline news from Asia is but a continuing part of that omniscient blueprint.

So, too, may the religions of Asia, when viewed from a Christian perspective, bring us to a greater understanding as to where man has strayed from the truth of God in the search for meaning in life. Such an understanding also leads not only to the formulation of a compassionate Christian response, but to a renewed appreciation of who Christ is in our own lives.

When we view Asia's colorful cultural mosaic through Christian eyes, we can take delight in how imaginative our Creator has been in designing such an interesting world. When we acquire a spiritual understanding of other peoples, we move thereafter with greater compassion, love, and consideration. Cultural differences become opportunities for sharing rather than being points of separation.

Spiritually, Asia represents one of today's great mission challenges. This is harvest season in Asia. As is true elsewhere in the world, the fire of the Holy Spirit is igniting the nations of Asia. From mud-walled villages in Bangladesh to gleaming skyscrapers in Singapore, the lordship of Jesus Christ is being proclaimed. Originally, the Asian continent was the birthplace of the world's great religions: Hinduism, Judaism, Buddhism, Christianity, and Islam. South Asia was later visited by Christian missionaries in the first century A.D. The Gospel of Jesus Christ then spread to the New World in the fifteenth and sixteenth centuries and finally to the interior of Africa in the nineteenth century.

Now, seemingly, the Gospel has gone full circle. Asia is economically, politically, and spiritually part of the wave of the future. Contemporary Christians in Asia and the West have the opportunity to utilize every means available to develop creative strategies for reaching Asia with the Gospel. Taking advantage of this opportunity calls for a deeply committed people, an earnestly praying people, and an informed people.

But first a note of caution. This book is not intended for the serious scholar of Asia; library card catalogs offer an overwhelming array of sources for such scholars. Nor is this book calculated to present a strictly Western viewpoint; a Christian perspective is not limited by geography or culture. Because the Holy Spirit carries no passport or visa, the Kingdom Culture which is being established worldwide transcends national boundaries.

Moreover, this book is a survey; that is, it necessarily touches on many topics but is not intended to discuss any single topic in depth. By necessity, the book moves from the general to the specific in order to establish a broad foundation from which to understand Asia today. For example, certain wider themes pertaining to much of the rest of the world also apply to Asia. Furthermore, specific Asian characteristics are inseparably linked together. Asia's history yields little meaning without some knowledge of its geography while Asia's contemporary culture is inextricably tied to its history. Furthermore, Asia's ancient religions are major determinents in events taking place today. Therefore, any attempt to understand Asia must regard Asia as a whole entity rather than as unrelated compartments.

Hopefully this book will serve to instill in each of us a greater sense of commitment to the urgent fulfillment of the Great Commission and a greater vision of what role each of us might play in that effort. Because modern technology has made our world so small, we can more easily become "world Christians"; that is, Christians who have a conscious sense of being part of a worldwide Christian fellowship, a Kingdom Culture, and whose prayer life and spiritual activities reflect a genuine commitment and heartfelt desire to assist in God's global plan to bring all people to Himself.

With these thoughts as a point of departure, let us look now at Asia as it exists within the larger context of what is usually termed the "Third World."

Chapter One

From Rice Paddies to Shanty Towns

A sleek Mercedes Benz with its back seat occupant staring straight ahead winds its way through a squalid section of Manila. A little girl in Calcutta busily makes patties from fresh cow dung on a day when she ought to be in school. Newspapers in Bombay announce that a young bride has mysteriously burned to death, the victim of the dowry system. In Jakarta, a newly arrived young man from some village wanders aimlessly through the streets looking for a job. In Dacca, an old woman lies dying from the effects of malnutrition, while in rural Thailand a rice farmer wonders how to sell his abundant crop. What do all of these people have in common? They are all Asians who share common problems with their counterparts in other Third World countries.

Within a larger context, Asia is best understood when viewed as part of the Third World. Presently there are exceptions of this within Asia, such as Japan, now a First World nation, as well as other areas which—as Newly Industrialized Countries (NIC's) like South Korea, Singapore, Hong Kong, and Taiwan—are moving out of the Third World category. But huge areas such as India, Pakistan, Bangladesh, China, and most of Southeast Asia are still considered to be part of the Third World.

Therefore certain Third World themes can be applied generally to Asia.

The term "Third World" was first used in the 1950's in France when political scientists began using labels for areas of world development. The "First World" refers to such industrialized and capitalist nations as those of Western Europe, the United States, Canada, Australia, New Zealand, and Japan. The "Second World," a term not so frequently used, refers to industrialized communist nations like the Soviet Union and Eastern Europe.

The "Third World" consists of those nations, primarily of Africa, Latin America, and Asia, whose economies are underdeveloped. In recent years, the term "Less Developed Country" (LDC) has gained popularity. On occasion the label "Two-Thirds World" also refers to the Third World. The developing nations of the world could actually be called "pre-developed" because many of them once were proud possessors of a high degree of development such as the Incan and Mayan civilizations of Latin America, the Mogul in India, and such great dynasties as the T'ang and Sung of China. With these varied suggestions in mind, the "Third World" might best be defined as that part of the world which has an unequal relationship with the developed world particularly in such areas as income, health standards, and education.

Rural Forces

When considering the Third World and Asia in particular, an outsider should keep in mind that approximately 60 percent of the workers of the Third World are engaged in agriculture. In some areas such as China, the figure runs as high as 80 to 85 percent. The percentage is more dramatic when it is compared to that in the United States where less than two percent of the working populace is employed in agriculture. Not only do most Third World people make their living from the soil, but they do so on very small parcels of land. Although the median size farm in the Third

World is five hectares or about twelve acres, many are much smaller.

Often a farmer in a developing nation is referred to as a peasant—a general term for one who works the land himself, earns his primary income from the soil and who may or may not own the land. He may be a tenant in an arrangement involving the exchange of his labor for the right to cultivate the land owned by another. In some areas, particularly of Latin America, he may be a sharecropper whose landowner provides seed and implements in exchange for a major share of the income.

In a peasant society, the household is the basic unit; all members of the family are involved in crop producing and harvesting. Large families are an asset rather than a liability, a fact that is often overlooked by non-agrarians when considering the controversial subject of overpopulation. A comfortable rhythm of life based upon the annual cycles of the seasons has existed unbroken for centuries. Local feast days and religious observances often relate to the cycles of planting and harvesting.

Within rural settings, kinship networks such as clans and tribes provide an important sense of security and identity. An interference in the delicate balance of the rhythm of rural life can be extremely upsetting, a fact the sensitive missionary will keep in mind.

While farmers all over the world are victims of difficulties often out of their control, Third World farmers are subject to the vicissitudes of the tropical climate. A glance at a world map reveals that a large portion of the Third World falls within an area 30 degrees north and south of the Equator. The Nobel Prize winning Indian poet Rabindranath Tagore once referred to the geographic plight of the tropics as the "tyranny of the tropics" for which the people forced to live there pay an almost intolerable price.

Rarely are tropical conditions moderate. Rainfall may come in a deluge or drought conditions may exist accompanied by soaring temperatures and high humidity. Such conditions sap the energy and reduce personal productivity of the Indian peasant winnowing his grain in the debilitating sun or the Malaysian woman gathering latex in a steamy plantation of rubber trees.

Not only must Third World farmers labor under the climatic burden of the tropics, but they are subject to an environment that frequently brings catastrophe their way. The Third World is more often than not in the geographic pathway of droughts, floods, typhoons, and tidal waves. Because of the location of the earth's plates and through the gradual process of continental drift, earthquake zones exist down the western side of Latin America, across the Pacific chain of islands, along the southern edge of the Himalayas, and into Turkey—all Third World areas. Little wonder that morning newspapers sometimes bring headlines of an earthquake in Guatemala or Mexico City, places where people are already living in impoverished circumstances.

Unfortunately, Third World inhabitants also have caused some of their own ecocatastrophes through unwise use of the land. Slash and burn agriculture, widely practiced in Third World nations, particularly in Africa, causes an increase in soil fertility during the first year but a drastic fertility decrease by the third year. This land is then abandoned and a new forest clearing is made. Not only is forest land being destroyed at an alarming rate, but the abandoned infertile fields are subject to leaching since there is nothing to hold precious nutrients in the soil. Not infrequently, the pressure of increased population forces peasants to use the fallow soil before it has had a chance to replenish itself.

Poor land management, particularly in Africa, has also led to the phenomenon of creeping deserts. Satellite photography reveals a measurable change in desert locations since the late 1970's. Everywhere from the Atlantic coast in Africa across the Sahel, into the Middle East, to Iran, Pakistan, and northwest India, the deserts are creeping ever larger. Man himself forms the catalyst for this ecocatastrophe. Farmers introduce cultivation into areas unsuited for agriculture while nomads expand herds beyond the capacity of the soil to maintain adequate pasture land.

Added to the problem of advancing deserts, Third World farmers must cope with pests such as tsetse fly and rinderpest little known by farmers of the developed world. Urban sprawl also contributes to the alarming fact that farmland all over the world is being lost at twice the rate that new lands are being opened. Thus landholdings become smaller and farmers, squeezed out, are forced to migrate to cities thereby contributing to overcrowding and urban sprawl. The cycle perpetuates itself.

Another ecological dilemma, particularly apparent in Asia, is the deforestation caused by the daily, unending search for firewood to be used as cooking fuel. Few women in industrialized societies give a thought to the source of their cooking fuel as they press the buttons of their electric stoves or microwave ovens.

Yet for women of the Third World the need for cooking fuel presents a daily problem. As nearby sources of wood are consumed, the search for firewood takes women and children farther and farther each day. In Nepal, children often walk for hours to bring back a precious bundle of wood from forests already being denuded. The loss of these valuable watersheds sets the stage for severe flooding, soil erosion, and creeping deserts. In some Pakistani towns even the bark has been stripped from trees. In Uganda, a family may spend as much as 30 percent of its income for firewood. No wonder ecologists are calling it the "other" energy crisis.

As an alternative to firewood, many Third World families, particularly in South Asia, have turned to the use of cow dung as a source of cooking fuel. A visitor to a South Asian village, town or even large city might be surprised to see children collecting fresh cow dung and plastering the hand-molded patties to walls to dry for later use. Of course, a more beneficial use of the cow dung would be as fertilizer; but when a choice has to be made between fertilizer and cooking fuel, the latter is made.

Are there solutions to this multitude of problems of the rural Third World? Solutions do exist but require the joint efforts of the developed world and the Third World. One solution is the so-called "Brown Revolution" in which land is redistributed from wealthy landowners to individual farmers. As a farmer tills his own land, his level of incentive rises remarkably as does his productivity. The greatly increased productivity of Taiwanese farmers following such a Brown Revolution is an outstanding example of this success. With the corresponding increase in a farmer's income, the housing, nutritional and health standards of his family can also rise. But the redistribution of land is not in itself successful unless it is accompanied by the availability of rural credit and by a more efficient marketing system.

Another solution to the farmers' problems has been the "Green Revolution." Begun in the 1960's, the Green Revolution involved the introduction of high yield variety seeds of rice and wheat into Asia, Africa and Latin America. Unquestionably the Green Revolution has been successful in some rural areas of the world, particularly in Southeast Asian rice production. But in order for the Green Revolution to be permanently successful elsewhere, certain problems must be dealt with. The high yield variety seeds require fertilizer, pesticides and great amounts of water--commodities that are not always available or affordable. Such increased production also requires greater mechanization, a factor which can force unemployed farmers into the cities (one tractor eliminates five agricultural jobs). Thus the jury is still in deliberation on the success of the Green Revolution.

Food production in the Third World has managed to keep slightly ahead of population growth and, in some areas such as Thailand, a surplus has even accumulated. The dire prediction made by the Rev.Thomas Malthus in 1798 that population growth would always outstrip the food supply has been averted at least temporarily. Despite food surpluses in some parts of the Third World, sizable areas remain where there is little available food or where there is starvation. The lack of transportation, roads, and money to purchase food have made for unequal distribution of food supplies.

There are other solutions for rural problems in the Third World. One that has been given considerable attention in recent years is known as "appropriate technology." This suggestion calls for the establishment of small scale industries at the village level. Called "cottage industries" by Mahatma Gandhi, such industries might include solar energy projects or bio-gas plants.

Other suggestions call for cottage industries such as handicrafts that can be sold outside the village. These cottage industries are designed not only to bring in additional income but to employ farmers during slack seasons or farmers who would otherwise be forced to migrate to cities. Such small scale industries utilize local resources and employ people rather than large machines. Examples exist in some villages of India such as a small scale silk industry or a carpentry industry making brightly painted wooden toys for export.

If such solutions offer some hope for success, they can be even more important when encompassed within a framework of Biblical Christianity that combines compassion and concern. Christian ethics is not just an ideal to be preached but one that can be translated into reality by the power of Jesus Christ to transform human lives. Translated into realistic terms, Christianity can bring about a sense of stewardship of the land that can help avert ecocatastrophes or can instill the motivation for pride in workmanship and more harmonious relationships at the village level simply because human hearts have been transformed.

Psalm 33:12 says "Blessed is the nation whose God is the Lord," suggesting that a whole nation is elevated when its people make the Lord their God. To uplift the life of one person is to uplift a whole nation. As the covenant-keeping God blesses each person who makes a commitment to Him, so a village, a city, and a whole nation is blessed.

Urbanization

As a person moves about, often with difficulty, through the crowded *favelas* of Sao Paulo or *bustees* of Calcutta, it becomes apparent that any strategy for missions must take into account another important trend in the Third World: urbanization. The annual rate of increase of the population in urban areas is three percent. At the present, some 20 percent of the persons in the Third World live in cities of over 20,000. Eight of the ten cities projected to have the largest population by the year 2000 are in the Third World with Mexico City (31,500,000) projected to be the largest.

With the exception of Latin America, this trend toward urbanization in the Third World is predominantly a male phenomenon. Women and children often stay behind on the land to farm it and to maintain a village base to which the men can return periodically. The urbanization of the developing world is also a phenomenon of the young, usually persons in their twenties or even late teens. The women who do migrate to cities are even younger. The impetus to urban migration is based upon economic considerations and also a level of rising expectations of a better life in cities.

So at a rate of 25,000 per day, these hopeful souls flock with their meager possessions to the burgeoning cities of the Third World, naively believing life will somehow be better. In all probability, these newcomers will become additional statistics of the unemployed or underemployed. Those who are fortunate enough to find work are likely to end up in one of the developing world's endless variety of small scale shops or sidewalk enterprises. There they eke out meager existences repairing, recycling or selling some small item. A single block in Calcutta might include, among other things, a tiny shop selling sweets, another selling plastic buckets, a bicycle repair shop, a barber shop, a tire shop, and a corner fruit vendor.

Accompanying this swollen population in Third World cities is a bloated bureaucracy, idealistically but ineptly attempting to administer some degree of order amid desks piled with stacks of yellowing paper. The frustration of a business transaction may drag on for weeks as papers are passed from one bespectacled and unsmiling bureaucrat to another.

As urban populations swell, so do the dimensions of the slums known in many languages from *barriadas* to *bustees* to *favelas.* Comprised of an amazing array of cardboard, scrap wood, flattened cans and bits of cloth, they may in reality be squatter settlements or shanty towns. The difference between the two is often not in appearance but in the fact that squatter settlements are built on the land illegally while the shanty towns are those sections on rented plots, sometimes even government-owned.

The trend toward urbanization should be born in mind by those interested in Christian missions. The human environment and habitat will be transformed from one in which a man who once had a comfortable kinship with the soil suddenly finds himself transplanted into a confusing, impersonal, and dehumanizing world. Urban ministries must be given greater importance as the human casualties of urbanization increase. Housing for the homeless, food for the hungry, medicine for the sick, comfort for the lonely, assurance for the confused comprise the increasing challenge of urban missions in the Third World.

The size of cities and the density of population can present a discouraging picture unless one compassionately sees the opportunity as does Mother Teresa and her Missionaries of Charity. When asked if she is perhaps overwhelmed by the size of the task, she replied that she does not think in terms of statistics but rather thinks of them "One at a time, one at a time." Jesus was moved with compassion when He saw the crowds but also set the example of patiently ministering one on one.

Chapter Two

Mud Huts and Blue Jeans

Traditionalism vs. Modernization

In Calcutta an exhausted rickshaw puller leans against the shaft of his antiquated vehicle while behind him a shop window advertises videotapes for home television use. In Shanghai Chinese doctors experimentally apply laser technology to the ancient techniques of acupuncture. In Karachi a camel lumbers slowly down a road as a new white Toyota whizzes past. These pictures and thousands more like them in Asia and the rest of the Third World form the mosaic of a very significant trend: the clash of traditionalism and modernization. This is a trend that is closely related to urbanization but which also reaches all the way down to the village level.

Traditionalism, the age-old pattern of doing things, offers security in anyone's life from the cradle to the grave. In a highly traditional society, such as commonly exists in the Third World, marriage is often arranged. The question of "Who shall I marry?" rarely arises since parents or go-betweens have already taken care of the issue. Following the traditional marriage celebration, the young couple usually goes to live with the groom's family. Little choice of job or occupation exists for those engaged in farming or whose family has for generations provided a skill or craft for the village. Sometimes a village can function with very little need for cash due to the barter system or a payment-in-kind arrangement.

In such traditional settings, roles are assigned: women play a subservient role, older men provide leadership and decision making while the role of younger men is somewhere in between. In many village settings, the daughter-in-law must be submissive to her mother-in-law, often until the birth of the first son. With assigned roles, the level of expectation is much lower and so, perhaps, is the level of frustration.

In a highly traditional society, one's marriage and possibly the birth of the first son are the two most exciting events of an otherwise monotonous and wearisome existence. Because of the weight tradition bears, such eventualities as illness, loss of abilities, and death are accepted as inevitable uncertainties.

Colliding head-on with the security of traditionalism in the Third World is the powerful force of modernization. Unquestionably modernization can bring with it numerous beneficial changes. Mechanization and technological advances increase production and provide a greater variety of finished products. Modernization in the Third World has been accompanied by improved health care and educational facilities as well as more highly developed infrastructures such as roads, bridges, canals and dams.

But the clash between traditionalism and modernization has jolted and destabilized whole societies. As traditional patterns are eroded, a corresponding blurring of roles takes place. Young women begin to question a system which keeps them in subservience. Generational discord mounts as young men migrate to cities or as young people scorn traditional customs such as arranged marriages.

What is happening worldwide is that a global village is being created in which the mode is western. The result is a Coca-cola and blue jean culture stretching from Kenya to Peru to Thailand. Modernization and westernization have become synonymous. Such westernization is a form of cultural imperialism which began with the European colonialism of the nineteenth century. Implicit within this new form of imperialism is the illusion that things western are somehow superior to things traditional. This sense is frequently accompanied by a form of humiliation in which the local elites of a Third World country feel embarrassed or ashamed by what they perceive as the backwardness of their own country.

After the withdrawal of white European-led governments in former colonies, the local elites filled the positions of power and influence. They not only assumed power but adopted western traditions and now are the carriers of western values in the new global village. This newly empowered class indulges in the conspicuous consumption that builds opulent homes, drives luxury automobiles, and sends children to exclusive European or American schools. Power in the Third World means wealth and status—wealth and status which must be displayed. Because of the display of such wealth, the plight of the poor becomes all the more striking. The opulent lifestyle of Ferdinand and Imelda Marcos, revealed after their departure from Manila, is an extreme example of such conspicuous consumption.

Accompanying the phenomenon of the global village is a rebellious spirit of youth in the Third World as they turn against their parents, the reminders of traditionalism. Fueled by the media including television, movies, music and radio, young people are introduced to the values and products of the developed world, a world that is primarily urban and non-traditional, a world far removed from the realities of their own environment. It is a world of fast cars or trendy clothes, a world of which they aspire to be a part and which they would like to wish into existence. In Asia one sees young people from New Delhi to Bangkok, from Kuala Lumpur to Manila, dressed in the international uniform—the blue jean and t-shirt. The *dhotis* and *sarongs* of their parents are gone, an outward symbol of their rejection of traditional values and customs.

Not only are western values encouraged by the media, but they are also perpetuated by multinational corporations (corporations with headquarters in the developed world and subsidiaries worldwide). Sometimes referred to as MNC's, giant companies such as Pepsico, Xerox and Gulf Western advertise and sell their products all over the world. Fast food restaurants and western products greet the surprised western visitor in almost every major city of the Third World. The tourist himself is a conveyor of western values. Not only is he well equipped with camera, matching designer luggage, and wad of travelers' checks, but more often than not, he insists upon maintaining his western comforts in a less developed country. In so doing, he further conveys the illusion of western superiority.

The result of these singularities of the global village is the creation of what has been referred to as the "expectation explosion." The level of rising expectations exceeds the nation's ability to fulfil those expectations. The result can be frustration, disillusionment, passivity, alienation, or violence.

An example of the creation of such an unfulfillable expectation occurred with the enunciation by the Chinese government in 1978 that China was embarking on the path of the Four Modernizations. In science and technology, defense, and agriculture the Chinese goal was to be equal with the developed countries by the year 2000.

Although remarkable economic progress has been made in China in the last five years, it has become apparent that the goal of the Four Modernizations is unrealistic. China lacks the specialized workers, managerial finesse, investment capital, foreign exchange, and efficient bureaucracy to accomplish such a lofty goal. The result of such unfulfilled expectations in China is that the Chinese have become passive unbelievers. More specifically, the youth of China grow increasingly alienated from and disenchanted with government promises.

Neo-Colonialism

Any attempt to understand the contemporary Third World, particularly Asia, must include a consideration of the experience of colonialism. Begun in the New World in the fifteenth and sixteenth centuries by Spain and Portugal, colonialism soon encompassed most of what is today the Third World. During its most aggressive phase, colonialism culminated in the "Scramble for Africa" in the 1880's and 1890's. Africa was carved up like a giant pie in which tribal boundaries and native considerations were ignored.

No European power approximated the empire-building of Great Britain whose possessions circled the globe. Within Asia alone, the British ruled Singapore, Malaysia, Hong Kong, a coastal area in China, Ceylon, Burma, and of course, India, the "jewel in the crown." Elsewhere in Asia, the major colonial powers were the French, who acquired Indochina, and the Dutch, who controlled Indonesia.

Why the imperial impulse to acquire overseas colonies? When the industrial revolution began transforming Western European lifestyle, the need for raw materials as well as markets for manufactured goods seemed greater than the risks of colonizing. The emphasis on large navies "He who rules the waves rules the world" was the order of the day.) required refueling stations around the globe. Added to these considerations was, of course, the power and prestige that came from being an imperial power.

But there were other, less measurable considerations. Advising America to acquire colonies after the Spanish-American War in 1898, Rudyard Kipling, poet of the British Empire, penned the famous words, "Take up the white man's burden." Implicit in his advice was the idea, common at the time, that the white man was not only superior but that he owed it to the future of mankind to spread his desirable civilization worldwide.

Missionaries took up the white man's burden. Although unquestionably some carried the prejudice of racial superiority, as a whole these early missionaries were fired by a spiritual zeal to take the Gospel to the ends of the earth. Most labored under unbelievable hardships that would daunt the missionary of today. While missionaries were not government-sponsored, European governments did on occasion back them with such military force as the joint expedition to rescue besieged missionaries in China during the Boxer Rebellion (1900).

Indisputably European colonialism left its enduring mark on the Third World. There were beneficial results like the establishment of hospitals and schools and the building of roads and canals. Not only did colonialism spread European culture to every hemisphere, but it also created a global economy from which developing nations have not yet fully recovered. Because the colonial powers were more interested in raw materials and markets, often-times one crop or natural resource was developed at the expense of secondary development. In Indochina, the French were solely interested in rubber, in Bolivia the Spanish wanted silver, in India the British wanted cotton and tea.

Such policies had far-reaching results. First, the colonial economies were, and in some cases still are, dependent upon international market prices for one crop or product. Second, prime agricultural land was diverted from food production to cash crops such as coffee or cocoa which have no nutritional value to the villagers nearby. Malaysia is an excellent example. Not only were large land areas given over to rubber plantations, but today the Malaysian economy must compete with synthetic counterparts to rubber. At a human level, this practice means that hundreds of Malaysian men, married and with families to support, sit idly during slumps when the rubber market is down.

Although the colonial powers granted independence to their former colonies, especially during the 1960's, a form of neo-colonialism soon became the replacement. Not only have wealthy nationals filled the power vacuum, but the economic dependency has continued through the mechanism of the multinational corporations (MNC's). Unfortunately, the bulk of the profits of the MNC's return home rather than remain to be used in the Third World countries for real development.

Human Underdevelopment

In any nation, rich or poor, it is people who constitute that nation's greatest resource and potential for the future. Often in the flood of Third World statistics and facts, the human dimension becomes lost. The weary mother in Bangladesh bent over her cooking fire in a mud-hut; the Chinese peasant woman, told by the government that she must have an abortion; the Philippine peasant toiling for a pittance in the heat of the day in the sugar cane fields—these and millions more like them are the ones Jesus came to redeem and to call unto Himself. These are the ones to whom Jesus says, "Come unto Me and I will give you rest."

Regrettably, the story in the Third World is that millions of people are the victims of human underdevelopment—people prevented from reaching their full God-given potential as human beings. Malnutrition, disease and poor education impede progress toward that fulfillment.

Perhaps no human affliction is as insidious and as widespread as malnutrition, a condition which saps the energy of the victim, deprives him of vitality and makes him vulnerable to a host of diseases. From 400 million to one billion people on planet Earth are malnourished, suffering from what Gandhi once referred to as the "eternal compulsory fast."

Among the specific forms of malnutrition is Protein Energy Malnutrition, a condition in which a lack of calories causes the body to burn up protein as fuel rather than use it for building body cells. Kwashiorkor is the advanced condition, usually found among children, in which the body is 20 to 30 percent underweight. The child's arms and legs become very thin, the belly grows swollen and distended, and the hair takes on a reddish hue. Malnutrition is most serious among children, particularly for those under the age of five; in their weakened conditions these little ones lack the defenses to fight off diseases or the ravages of diarrhea. Thus they easily succumb to diseases which, to children of the developed world, would rarely be fatal.

Among adults, a common nutritional affliction is anemia, a serious iron deficiency which strikes as many as two-thirds of the women and one-third of the men of the Third World. For religious reasons or because of lack of an insufficient supply of meat or fish, they may eat vegetarian diets and thus not receive sufficient amounts of iron in their diets. Both children and adults are victims of severe Vitamin A deficiency a lack which leads to defective vision, an untreated plight of countless Third World persons.

One of the saddest forms of malnutrition, and perhaps the most easily cured, is the nutritional deficit that afflicts the infant who is weaned too early. From ages six months to two years the infant's resistance to disease is at its lowest point--hence the need for breast milk with its built-in capacity to ward off disease. No more nutritious diet exists for babies and, best of all, it is absolutely free.

Yet many Third World mothers are led to believe that instant or canned milk formulas are superior to breast milk. They identify the western product with the promise of good health for their babies and see the use of it as a status symbol, an image promoted by the manufacturers of infant milk formula.

Unfortunately, use of such formulas is costly and dependent upon the availability of clean water, a luxurious commodity in the Third World. The use of impure water in mixing the formula and the likelihood of watering it down to make it last longer are harbingers of disease and malnutrition for the baby.

Close companion to malnutrition in the developing world is disease, an almost constant specter in the lives of the poor. Without adequate medical care they languish in squalid housing or even on the streets. Moreover, the diseases of persons in the developing world are almost unknown to the industrialized world. Typhoid, cholera, and leprosy have long received attention from colonial powers and international aid agencies.

But far more prevalent, although not necessarily fatal, are afflictions such as hookworm and threadworm, whose estimated victims number over a billion. Schistosomiasis, the waterborne parasite contacted by the quarter of a billion people who work with their feet in water, is one of the most common debilitating diseases in the world. The same is true of onchocerciasis, or river blindness, caused by the blackfly; this dread disease afflicts over 30 million people per year.

The battle against disease is further complicated by the lack, both in quantity and quality, of pure water. Fetching water may occupy several hours of every day for a woman or her children. Quite likely the water may be from a river or lake contaminated by human and animal wastes or by runoff from fertilizers or pesticides. Each year an estimated ten million persons in the Third World die from conditions related to impure water. Diarrheal disease, which debilitates life and leads to a painful death, is not only directly related to impure water but is also one of the most common of Third World afflictions.

Finally, another source of human underdevelopment in the less developed countries is poor education. A nation's literacy rate is one of the measurements of its well-being since education can become the answer to a multitude of problems. Some Third World nations such as China have made amazing strides in the battle against illiteracy. Illiteracy, the result either of poor education or of none at all, is part of a vicious cycle from which there seems to be little escape. Because a man is poorly educated, he is trapped in an illiterate world of poverty and because he is poor, he cannot afford an education. The illiteracy rate is highest in Africa and, throughout the Third World, is always highest among women.

From the beginning, children of poverty have several

strikes against developing their full educational capacities. If, as is likely, they have nutritional deficiencies, they may have some learning disabilities. Moreover, because of their impoverished living conditions, there is little in their home environment to stimulate imagination so necessary to develop learning abilities.

If these children of the poor are able to attend elementary school, their attendance may be interrupted when they work in the fields, factories, or at home. Secondary schools are usually located in cities where village children not only must leave home to study but also have money for board, uniforms, and books. This educational system has a built-in bias against the children of the poor. For these impoverished children, there is no transitional period such as that in the developing world identified as a "teenager," with all its accompanying carefree activities. Children of the Third World move from childhood to adulthood with no bridge to ease moving from one stage to the next.

In literally every country of the world, whatever its level of development, children are an endangered group for reasons ranging from abortion to child abuse and from prostitution to factory labor. Children are at the mercy of an adult world that uses them as possessions or pawns. Over 100 million youngsters are street children wandering in the hostile world of the survival-of-the fittest in such places as Bogota or New Delhi.

Estimates run as high as 200 million children under age sixteen working for wages outside the home. The largest group is employed in agriculture where such activity (which also keeps them out of school) often is not viewed as exploitative. In India, which has more child workers than any other country, children as young as five years of age break their bodies as they labor in textile mills, stone quarries, and brass factories, all for the equivalent of pennies a day.

Along the brightly lit streets of Manila, Bangkok, or Bombay the empty faces of child prostitutes number into the thousands. Some are only a few weeks removed from village settings where they became pawns to agents or moneylenders. In the bewildering cities they soon become hardened by the exploitation of foreign visitors from the United States, Japan, Australia, and Europe. Few will ever see their families again.

Finally, the women of the Third World are twice poor: first because they are born into the Third World and second because they are born female. In cities from Lima to Cairo, from Bombay to Bangkok, the observer sees smartly dressed, educated young women working in secretarial or clerical jobs. But for every woman in such fortunate circumstances, there are thousands of her counterparts who are enduring lives of endless hard work and grueling circumstances.

For the women of the developing world, the two primary tasks of house care and child rearing are the same as they are for women of the rest of the world. But added to these at the village level are such daily responsibilities as searching for firewood, carrying water, and grinding flour. These three tasks alone may take up half a woman's waking hours. In a traditional society, part of her woman's role may also include weeding and harvesting. Her work may increase if a male in the household migrates to the city. In many developing nations, particularly in South Asia, a woman is little more than a possession for whom life holds little cheer.

Not only is her life arduous, but is circumscribed by cultural and legal restrictions. The customs of dowries and bride prices discriminate against poor families or families with many daughters. In spite of the fact that the dowry system has been declared illegal, tradition dies slowly. In New Delhi alone, estimates suggest that two young brides die of burns every day, tragic victims of the dowry system. The groom's family, unhappy with the bride and seeking a girl with a larger dowry, arrange for a "cooking accident" that takes the life of yet another girl.

Furthermore, arranged marriages give the bride little

say about whom she will marry. Few women of the Third
World have the right to own land. Any legal proceedings
would be almost unheard of as her world is limited by illiteracy, a condition of approximately 60 percent of the
women of the Third World. Finally, her plight becomes almost hopeless in some African or South Asian societies
when she is widowed and thus becomes a cast-off. No
wonder Hindu women pray, "God, in my next life make me
a boy."

The Christian Response

To the problems created by the clash of traditionalism and
modernization, Christianity makes a relevant response. At
a time when young people are disillusioned with unfulfilled
promises or are discovering the hollowness of western
materialism, the Gospel of Jesus Christ offers a Savior who
is ". . . the same yesterday, today and forever." (Hebrews
13:8) In His sinless life, Jesus was and is all that he said He
would be. To the older generation, wondering what is
happening to the bedrock of their traditional societies,
Jesus is the Rock of Salvation. The Psalmist declares "The
Lord is my rock, my fortress and my deliverer." (ch.18,v.2)
To every people of every age, of every nation and every
culture, in a time of uncertainty, He is the One who said, "I
am the Lord; I change not." (Malachi 3:6) No greater
certainty exists.

From a Christian perspective, the Bible has some
compelling words to say in the book of Amos about the
issue of social injustice and the misuse of wealth. The book
was written in the eighth century B.C. when Israel was
spiritually smug, prosperous, and seemingly secure but
religiously and morally corrupt. The primary theme of this
important Old Testament book is the call to social justice.
In ch. 2:6,7, judgment is pronounced against Israel's op-
pression of the poor and the denial of justice: " . . . they
trample on the heads of the poor as upon the dust of the
ground and deny justice to the oppressed." In chs. 5,11,12,

the prophet exposes the misuse of wealth to build stone mansions rather than to help the poor. Finally, in ch. 8:4-7, Amos declares the Lord does not forget injustice and exploitation: " . . . I will not forget anything they have done." These were solemn words 27 centuries ago. They still are.

Can Christianity as a spiritual and moral force address the problems of human underdevelopment? The answer is a resounding "yes." The demonstration of compassion by Christians around the world stands out as one of the most impressive characteristics separating Christianity from other religions. Obviously there is a great deal more to be done.

The God of the prophet Isaiah declared, "Is not this the kind of fasting I have chosen: to loose the chains of injustice and untie the cords of the yoke, to set the oppressed free and break every yoke? Is it not to share your food with the hungry and to provide the poor wanderer with shelter, when you see the naked, to clothe him?" (ch. 58, v. 6-7)

If the teachings of Jesus Christ were put into action, the response would most certainly be concerned with disease, malnutrition and the plight of women and children. Jesus' strong words in Matthew 25:35-46 established the Christian standard for treatment of those who are sick, hungry, and naked. "For I was hungry and you gave me something to eat, I was thirsty and you gave me something to drink, I was a stranger and you invited me in, I needed clothes and you clothed me, I was sick and you looked after me, I was in prison and you came to visit me(v. 35,36) . . . whatever you did for one of the least of these brothers of mine, you did for me." (v. 40)

The Gospel of Jesus Christ is not proclaimed just in words but in deeds as well. There needs to be a groundswell of Christian indignation at the injustice and exploitation of those who cannot help themselves. Radical responses such as paying children to go to school may be needed. Granted the numbers are overwhelming, but to help one child is to make a start.

It has been rightly suggested that "hungry stomachs have no ears." The message of Christ must not only offer hope of eternal life but it must also be accompanied by the tangible promise of a better life here on earth. In James 1:27 we are told that pure religion that is acceptable to the Father includes looking after orphans and widows. Making provision for the less fortunate and those who cannot help themselves is a principle begun in the Old Testament. Perhaps the first command to take care of the poor was in Numbers 19:10 when the Lord commanded "Do not go over your vineyard a second time or pick up the grapes that have fallen. Leave them for the poor and the alien."

Finally, Christianity has made a difference in the status of women despite arguments of feminists to the contrary. By virtue of His very actions in talking with women on an equal basis such as in the example of the Samaritan woman at the well (John 4:7-26), or that of giving recognition to the sinful woman anointing His feet (Luke 7:37-50), Jesus was elevating the status of women. Paul instructs men to love their wives as they would their own bodies (Eph.5:28). As an illustration of the difference Christianity can make, a young man from New Guinea whose entire village had become Christian, commented "We now esteem our women" Into the hopeless cycle of despair in Third World women, Jesus brings the warmth of His singularly potent love and the bright hope of life eternal.

Very simply stated, the redemptive power of God changes human hearts. When human hearts are changed, a transformation occurs which is then reflected in the institutions, organizations, and communities of mankind. Systemic change can take place but only when a fallen world is changed. God's blueprint is to redeem a fallen world and His method is to transform individual human hearts through His love. That is the hopeful message to a needy world.

Chapter Three

The Monsoon's Gift

A Geographic Perspective

The Psalmist pays tribute to the Master Geographer in Psalms 102:25-26 when he writes: "In the beginning you laid the foundations of the earth, and the heavens are the work of your hands. They will perish, but you remain; they will all wear out like a garment. Like clothing you will change them and they will be discarded. But you remain the same, and your years will never end."

As we spy out the land known as Asia, we discover that so large is Asia that if one holds the globe in a certain direction, Asia is all that can be seen. Asia seems so immense that it is hard to believe such a great land mass could perish, but the Word tells us that even the earth will wear out. Only its majestic Creator remains the same.

With the Himalaya Mountains forming a great, snowy spine across it, Asia spans an incredible area of 17,000 miles from the Pacific in the east to the Ural Mountains in the west. Its connection with Africa is broken only at the Isthmus of Suez and the connection broken with North America by the narrow Bering Strait. Geographically, Asia includes Soviet Asia as well as Southwest Asia, sometimes called the Middle East. Because of marked cultural differences and geographic distinctions, neither of these Asian regions will be discussed in this book.

The Monsoon

When most people think of Asia, they quite likely think of both a geographic and cultural area which is more accurately referred to as "Monsoon Asia." This popular image pictures that part of Asia including South Asia, Southeast Asia and the Far East which lies in the geographic pathway of either the summer or winter monsoon. This annual weather cycle, sometimes known as the "life breath of Asia," irrigates the precious cropland of some three billion people.

During the summer, from May to September, winds bring the rain from oceans that quench a vast land area from Japan to India. Because the land heats faster than the water, moist air is pulled, creating a motion that forces clouds to release their moisture. The winter monsoon reverses this process. Cold winds sweep down across China bringing dry air to much of Asia but bringing rains to Indonesia and Australia. This annual cycle, so eagerly awaited by millions of Asian farmers, can avert famine. However, as the monsoon season reaches its peak, that same cycle can often be the harbinger of human misery and suffering when floods wash away whole villages in Bangladesh or when families in Thailand attempt to carry on daily life with flood waters inundating an entire nation.

Throughout Asia, the largest concentrations of population live in alluvial regions where rivers have deposited rich soil, particularly during flood season. The intensive agriculture possible in such areas has supported high population densities. The best examples of such regions in Asia are the Indus Valley in India and Pakistan, the Irawaddy in Southeast Asia, and the Yellow and Yangtze Rivers in China

South Asia

South Asia includes India, Pakistan, Bangladesh, Nepal, Bhutan, and Sri Lanka. In India, along the Ganges River, dwells an enormous mass of people in what is the second largest population cluster in the world. (Japan ranks as the most densely populated area in the world.) South Asia could be called a peninsula were it not for the massive size that makes it more accurately called a subcontinent. Isolated from the rest of Asia by the great wall of the Himalayas, South Asia is bounded also by the Arabian Sea, the Indian Ocean, and the Bay of Bengal. No wonder that a distinctive, although heterogeneous, culture developed in South Asia.

Newspaper headlines announce South Asia's religious problems almost weekly. For it is in South Asia that some of the strongest regionalism in the world exists, not because of geography, but because of differing religious beliefs. Hindus attack Muslims in northern India, while in Sri Lanka the strife between Hindus and Buddhists drags on month after month. The religious configuration of South Asia appears like a crazy quilt design. Eighty-three per cent of India's population is Hindu, while Pakistanis are Islamic, the Bangladesh populace is split between Hindu and Islamic beliefs, and Sri Lankans are predominantly Buddhist with a Hindu minority.

Furthermore, as in any country any place in the world, inevitably two forces are at work: centrifugal forces which threaten to divide a nation and centripetal forces which bind a nation together. A nation's historical events supply evidence of these forces at work. India is an excellent example of these forces existent within one society. Her religious configuration threatens to divide the nation into separate enclaves. In addition to the 83 per cent who are Hindu, 11 per cent are Muslim, two per cent are Christian, two per cent are Buddhist, and the remainder are Jain, Parsee or Sikh. Added to these centrifugal forces in India are the existence of over 3,000 castes, some 845 languages, and 1600 dialects!

Yet, amazingly, India somehow hangs together. Among the centripetal forces that seem to bind India together are political and religious strengths. From the dig-

nified capitol building in New Delhi to the councils of men
sitting under trees in villages, Indian democracy is a precious possession jealously guarded. Ironically, while
religious forces could splinter India, the very strength of
Hinduism helps bind the nation together. Hinduism (see
ch.6) is a great cultural force in India, a nation dotted with
holy places. Hinduism is not simply a religion but a whole
way of life shared by a majority of Indians.

Out of the nation of India, the British carved two
pieces of land in 1947 and made a separate nation:
Pakistan. The ill-conceived idea ended in 1972 when the
two parts severed ties to form separate nations, Pakistan
and Bangladesh. Today the very name "Bangladesh"
invokes a mental image of poverty. The unfortunate victim
of geography and civil strife, Bangladesh struggles to exist
against seemingly insurmountable odds.

Located on the flood plain of the Ganges River,
Bangladesh can count on flooding in August and September as the monsoon rains pour out their final fury. Added
to this is the tragic fact that Bangladesh also rests in the
geographic pathway of another of nature's rage—the
cyclone. In 1970, a cyclone with accompanying tidal wave
struck Bangladesh in what may have been one of the
greatest natural disasters of this century. An estimated
600,000 persons perished in addition to the devastation of
livestock, cropland, and housing.

Because of the frequent flooding, rice yields are low
while population density is extremely high. Statistics tell
the unfortunate story of Bangladesh: annual per capita income is $152 (1985), the average life expectancy is 49
years (compared with 74 in Hong Kong), and the literacy
rate is 26 per cent. About half the population suffers from
a deficiency of daily calories.

Not only is Bangladesh a victim of geography, but has
also gone through the divisive experience of two ruinous
and extremely bloody civil wars. When India was partitioned in 1947, Muslims and Hindus fled across borders
while bloody massacres took place on both sides. Again in

1972, Muslim-Hindu strife broke out, strife that resulted in an estimated death toll of 3,000,000. East Pakistan (1947) and Bangladesh (1972) were both born in the midst of strife from which Bangladesh has never fully recovered.

While Bangladesh has languished, Pakistan has fared somewhat better. United by the strength of Islam, it has not suffered from the religious strife of its former partner. Whereas Bangladesh is plagued by floods, Pakistan more often struggles with drought. With the installation of expanded irrigation networks, the nation's output of cotton has led to textile exports. More recently, however, poor weather conditions and insect infestations have brought about a marked drop in agricultural production.

Finally, the island nation of Sri Lanka, formerly Ceylon, is also considered a part of South Asia. As a result of almost four hundred years of European influence, Sri Lanka has a highly developed plantation economy based upon tea and rubber. What makes Sri Lanka unusual in South Asian terms is that it is neither predominantly Hindu nor Muslim. About 70 per cent of the Sri Lankans are Sinhalese Buddhists, the ethnic descendants of early Aryan invaders.

When the British ruled Ceylon, they encouraged the darker skinned Dravidians to migrate to Ceylon from India to work on the plantations. These people spoke Tamil and practiced the Hindu religion. Today, Sri Lanka reaps a harvest of bitterness and bloodshed from the ethnic and religious diversity resulting from that migration. As newspaper headlines remind the world, the Sri Lankan strife goes on with no real resolution in sight.

Southeast Asia

Two geographic features of Southeast Asia present a formidable challenge to the missionary. First, this region's location places it between two giants, India and China, a fact which has heavily influenced Southeast Asian history. Second, a glance at the map shows the degree to which

Southeast Asia is fragmented. Best described as a peninsula of peninsulas with scattered islands offshore, the area is mountainous and blanketed with a tropical rain forest. Population is concentrated in river valleys, in coastal plantation areas, or in those mountainous areas such as Java where rich volcanic soil invites intensive cultivation.

In terms of ethnicity and culture, Southeast Asia defies definition because of her numerous ethnic, linguistic, and religious groups, each of which presents special challenges to the sharing of the Gospel. The mainland area is composed of seven separate nations including Burma, Thailand, Malaysia, Singapore, Kampuchea, Laos, and Vietnam. Also considered part of Southeast Asia are the island nations of Indonesia, the Philippines, and Brunei (located on the Indonesian island of Borneo).

The diversity of Southeast Asia is dramatically revealed through the literally hundreds of distinct languages and dialects spoken throughout the region. Rarely do all the people within a Southeast Asian nation speak a common language. To add to the fragmentation, getting from one place to another must often be accomplished by water, utilizing an amazing array of crafts, ranging from ferries to motorized boats to dugout canoes. Overland transportation is tedious over long, perilously narrow, winding roads that thread their way through dense tropical forests and over mountain ranges.

Despite the great diversity of Southeast Asia, two common characteristics exist throughout the region: the tropical climate and a rice-based agricultural system. The term "paddy" can mean "unhusked rice," but it also refers to the flooded fields where rice is grown. Some 50 per cent of the land of Southeast Asia produces as many as 3,000 different varieties of rice.

Although Southeast Asia is predominantly rural, one glaring exception is Singapore, a multi-ethnic, multi-religious city-state. Singapore is virtually the only nation in the tropics that has managed to raise the standard of living of its people above that of the developing nations. A newly industrialized nation, Singapore is now a major Asian center for manufacturing and commerce. With ultra-modern skyscrapers, tree-lined residential areas, fashionable shopping malls, and a highly literate, cosmopolitan populace, Singapore represents a unique challenge in urban missions strategy.

While Singapore continues its dynamic economic growth, the majority of Southeast Asian nations, such as Laos, Vietnam, Kampuchea, and Indonesia, struggle against those problems characteristic of the Third World. Thailand and Malaysia represent nations in transitional stages, both having large rural populations, modern primary cities, rich natural resources, and, with time, the possibility of new economic growth.

East Asia

When most people think of Asia, their mental image quite likely focuses upon East Asia, also known as the "Orient" or the Far East. Dominated geographically and culturally by China, the region also includes the two Koreas, Japan, Taiwan, and Hong Kong. While these countries are fast becoming dynamic, separately viable entities, their past has been largely influenced by the Asian giant, China.

The home of an almost incomprehensibly large population of one billion, China's history is one of isolation imposed by her geography. Bordered by the Gobi desert to the north and west, the Himalayas in the south, and the China Sea to the east, China made little contact with the rest of the world. Her population has always been concentrated in what was sometimes called "China Proper," the area between the Yellow, Yangtze, and Pearl Rivers. Human labor was used to dig a thousand mile canal to connect the Yellow and the Yangtze.

Over the centuries, an elaborately built irrigation system in China Proper has made possible extremely intensive agriculture. The produce from agriculture, along with its related trade, led to an extensive and sometimes complicated marketing network that has existed for hundreds of years and played a significant role in Chinese life. From thousands of villages the network culminated in a hierarchy of China's largest cities and thus integrated China into a nation. However, somewhat out of the marketing system was the area northeast of the Yellow River, China's industrial belt—an area of coal mines, iron reserves, and large scale manufacturing. This traditional separation is now breaking down as China is making a concerted effort to distribute industrial sites around the country.

Aside from China Proper, which is the rice bowl area, China has vast areas that are less productive agriculturally. To the far northwest lie the desert basins of Xinjiang where an oasis program allows for cotton and wheat production. Sizable oil fields located here have given the area strategic importance. To the southwest lie the awesome snow-covered mountains and the high plateaus of Tibet where the average elevation is a mind-numbing 15,000 feet. Desolate, barren, and windswept, the region has gained recent importance because of the discovery of oil and coal reserves. Finally, the plateau steppe of Mongolia is characterized by searingly hot summers and bleak cold winters that do little to invite settlement except by the hardiest nomadic peoples.

Perhaps one of Asia's most alluring nations is Hong Kong, the setting for novels that conjure up Suzy Wong images of intrigue and exotic adventure. Located at the estuary of the Pearl River below Guangzhou (Canton), Hong Kong represents an enticing blend of East and West. Its 400 square miles are comprised of Hong Kong Island, the Kowloon Peninsula and, adjacent to China, the New Territories. Hong Kong's major importance long has derived from its excellent deep-water harbor which attracts ships from all over the world. Although its populace is 99 per cent Chinese, Hong Kong has been a British Crown Colony since 1841, an arrangement which will change in 1997 when Hong Kong reverts back to mainland Chinese rule. (See ch. 11)

Incredibly, some five million people jam into Hong Kong's small area of varied high-rise buildings. Government-built, high-rise apartment buildings, known as "estates," can house as many as 30,000 people. Each estate represents a self-contained mission field with a multitude of human problems.

Hong Kong has long been an anomaly of existence. With its thousands of small specialty shops contrasting with international offices of multi-million dollar corporations, Hong Kong is a bastion of capitalism located on the edge of a huge socialist power. Yet the colony depends upon China for its food and water. In addition to its busy port, Hong Kong is a major world financial center and a manufacturer of light industry, particularly of electronics, toys, and textiles.

Another East Asian nation, and a major exporter of textiles, is the island nation of Taiwan. Formerly known as Formosa, Taiwan was founded in 1949 as the Republic of China when some 2,000,000 refugees fled from the communist takeover on mainland China. Led by their Nationalist leader Chiang Kai-shek, the refugees crossed the 120 mile Formosa Strait. As a result of a very high birth rate (which now has been significantly slowed), Taiwan's population has reached approximately 20,000,000 in just over three decades.

Today, Taiwan is the economic envy of Asia. An ambitious land redistribution (Brown Revolution) program awarded nearly 95 per cent of Taiwan's farmers with land of their own. Although Taiwan still must import some foodstuffs, the Green Revolution has been very successful in a climate conducive to double cropping. With a high per capita income by Asian standards and a very high literacy rate, the Taiwanese have become an East Asian model of efficiency in a nation now classified as one of the Newly Industrialized Countries of the Pacific Rim.

Also considered one of the NIC's of the Pacific Rim is South Korea. In 1945, the Korean peninsula was divided at the 38th Parallel into North and South Korea. Although the people of the peninsula are unified ethnically and linguistically, there the similarity ends. Very little trade or exchange of any kind takes place between the two nations, a matter for great prayer by Christians who long to share the Gospel with their northern neighbors. North Korea's links with the outside world are primarily with China and the Soviet bloc countries.

The mountainous north produces only one crop per year, while the south, with its peninsular climate, is conducive to double cropping. Because of large coal deposits and the availability of hydroelectric power, heavy industry is concentrated in North Korea while South Korea relies upon the production of textiles and on lighter industry.

Miraculously South Korea has managed to overcome the destruction which resulted from the Korean War. Bolstered by foreign aid, especially from the United States, South Korea has harnessed its greatest resource, its people, into an efficient system of production. Buoyed by the expansion of the steel industry and by liberal economic programs, South Korea now ranks as one of Asia's most forward-looking countries.

However, of all Asian countries, Japan stands in a class by itself. Non-western, yet an urbanized, industrial giant, Japan is a marvel of modernization and efficiency. The nation consists of four main islands: the northern frontier island of Hokkaido, the heavily populated island of Honshu, and the southern islands of Kyushu and Shikoku.

By world estimates, Japan has long been a densely populated nation. As early as 1600, the capital city of Edo (now Tokyo) was the largest city in the world. Today the Tokyo-Yokohama megalopolis has the largest population of any metropolitan area in the world. Yet the Kanto Plain on which Tokyo and Yokohama are located also has extensive farming areas, a tribute to the Japanese talent for utilizing every square foot of available land in a nation where only one-fifth of the land can be cultivated. Nevertheless Japan's rice yields of 110 bushels per acre (U.S.

yields average 51 bushels per acre, China's are 35 bushels per acre) are the highest in the world. An age-old system of terracing, multiple cropping, and transplanting allows maximum use of a small amount of land.

Consequently Japan can produce about two-thirds of its own food needs even though the number of farmers is diminishing and consists to a considerable extent of elderly persons, especially women. The Japanese diet also depends upon fish which come from fish farms or from offshore fishing in international waters. Japan's fishing industry stands second only to that of the Soviet Union.

The distinctive genius of Japanese tradition has been a remarkable ability to adopt ideas from other cultures and adapt these to fit the Japanese character, whether that be Portuguese muskets in the sixteenth century or department stores (depato) of the twentieth century. Alongside this adaptive capacity exists a creative genius that is often a source of amazement and fascination to the rest of the world.

Yet the Japanese have been hampered by two persistent weaknesses—one quite obvious, the other less apparent. Although Japan has coal deposits, it greatly depends upon the importation of raw materials, especially iron ore and petroleum. Despite this dependency, however, its highly disciplined and efficiently organized systems of production have resulted in exports that have led to a huge trade surplus.

The second weakness of contemporary Japan is less definable and evolves from geographic as well as historic roots. For almost three hundred years, prior to 1868, the Japanese closed their doors to the outside world and remained a feudal society isolated from the rest of the world. Although Japan made a concerted effort to modernize after 1868, the sense of those lost years of isolation have lingered for decades.

But the sense of isolation has also been fostered by the insular character of Japan's geography. Influence from the outside world notwithstanding, the Japanese have traditionally held a sense of their own uniqueness that at times is characterized by a certain reserve and hesitancy to become involved in world affairs. Nevertheless, Japan now stands as one of the three or four major economic powers of the world.

Geopolitics

Like the other continents of the world, Asia has its portion of geopolitics—circumstances in which geographic factors determine political situations. For example, the existence of refugees as a result of a war is always a geopolitical circumstance. Such is the case in Pakistan where, as a result of the 1979 Soviet invasion of Afghanistan, hundreds of thousands of refugees have poured across Pakistan's northwest border seeking refuge. An estimated one-quarter of Afghanistan's 15,000,000 people have fled their homeland, some 3,000,000 of them to Pakistan. There these refugees, possessing only what they could carry, live in several hundred overcrowded camps run by the United Nations and mission agencies. Unlike refugees of Southeast Asia, the Afghan refugees have not found new homes in other countries. Nor do they want to. Their hope of returning home to Afghanistan is kept alive by their faith in the *mujahidin* (holy fighters), Muslim guerilla fighters.

For Christians, the plight of the Afghan refugees represents an opportunity to minister to the basic needs of a displaced people. In particular, the needs of fatherless children and of widows predominate in the camps. In Psalms 68:5, David gives praise to God as being a "... father to the fatherless and a defender of widows." Such a promise takes on tangible form through the work of Christian missions in refugee camps. Not only should Christians pray for the peace of Afghanistan but also for ways in which a hurting and needy people, predominantly Muslim in faith, can be reached. The financial burden of refugee ministries is especially great for those missions involved and provides a worthwhile opportunity for Christian generosity.

But Pakistan also has other border problems. Her border, shared to the east with India, has long been an area of unrest. The Kashmir region has been the object of distrust between India and Pakistan ever since the border was drawn up by the British in 1947. Kashmir, a magnificently picturesque area in northern India, is 75 per cent Muslim but ruled by Hindus in what is yet another area of the world torn by religious strife. Pakistan has openly aided Muslims in their fight against Indian-supported Hindus. A cease-fire line was drawn by the United Nations but is a shaky peace at best and represents the cause of ongoing disagreements between the Pakistani and Indian governments as well as requires a sizeable expenditure of money and manpower for defense.

However, a more immediate crisis for India is the interreligious strife taking place in the Punjab where the 1947 boundary line forced both Sikhs and Hindus to scramble to India while Muslims fled to Pakistan. Punjab state, located in northwest India, has become a prosperous agricultural region in which the Green Revolution appears to be very successful. The Punjab state is also the stronghold of the Sikh religion (a syncretic faith of Hindu and Muslim elements). From their holy city at Amritsar, Sikh militants have declared the founding of a separate Sikh nation, Khalistan. Bloody clashes between Sikhs and Hindus have erupted throughout India despite efforts to bring about a compromise. The most blatant Sikh attack came in the form of the assassination of Prime Minister Indira Gandhi in 1984 by her Sikh bodyguard. To allow Sikh separatism might trigger the separatist aspirations of other minority groups of Indians, including Christians in Nagaland.

Separatist aspirations are also the goal of the minority Hindu Tamils in Sri Lanka who are locked in bitter religious strife with their Sinhalese Buddhist neighbors. At-

tempts by India to intervene to bring about a peaceful settlement for the civil strife have only brought a no-win
situation to the Indian government.

In other areas of Asia, geography and politics are intertwined. Mainland China has long maintained that
Taiwan rightfully belongs to the mainland government and
that Beijing is the legitimate capital of all the Chinese. In
Korea, the 1953 United Nations truce line at the 38th
Parallel is another area of Asian instability. Peace is maintained only by an international force of the United Nations
stationed along the Demilitarized Zone. Proposals to
break the more than three decades of deadlock over the
divided peninsula have been repeatedly rejected by one
side or the other.

Elsewhere, in Southeast Asia, the geopolitical
circumstance is one of fragmentation, most markedly in
Indonesia and the Philippines. Indonesia consists of over
13,000 islands which comprise a unique blend of religions
and cultures which make governing difficult. Specifically,
secessionist uprisings have taken place in the Moluccan
Islands of Indonesia as people of the outer islands resent
Javanese domination of Indonesian affairs. Nevertheless,
Indonesian unity amidst diversity is, like that of India, a
centripetal force that binds the nation together, a nation in
which the Gospel of Jesus Christ is spreading rapidly.

In the Philippines, the geographic fragmentation is
easily recognized in the fact that the nation consists of over
7,000 islands. Secessionist emotions are strongest on the
southern island of Mindanao where a large concentration
of Muslims live. There, a militant group of Muslims resents
domination by predominantly Catholic Manila and
threatens to be as great a problem to the Aquino government as the communist insurgency. (see ch.11)

Another Southeast Asian geopolitical circumstance is
the displacement, since 1975, of some 1.6 million
Indochinese who have become refugees as a result of the
long-term political strife in the region. Although the UN

has helped some 85,000 Vietnamese to leave their country through its "Orderly Departure Program," the number of victims who have lost their lives in tragic attempts to escape by sea may never be known. A large number of Cambodian, Laotian, and Vietnamese refugees exists within the territory of Thailand where mission organizations estimate some 500,000 are presently living in camps and where aid from international agencies is declining.

Thus, a Christian perspective of Asia must include a consideration of the importance of geographic factors in so large a land mass. A survey of Asian geography and the political factors that result from its geography reveal many challenges to mission strategy in approaching such problems as fragmentation, insularity, and inhospitable climatic conditions.

But such a glance also reveals many intercessory prayer needs which can be met by Christians all over the world who need go no farther than their prayer closets. Every day lives are lost because of religious strife in Sri Lanka between Hindus and Buddhists, while in the Punjab Sikhs attack Hindus. In Afghan and Thai refugee camps, hundreds of thousands of homeless people languish in a state almost forgotten by the rest of the world. On the Korean peninsula, thousands of families, including many Christians, pray for the day when the specter of war will be removed. On Mindanao, Islamic insurgency sporadically threatens the lives of Christians, including Christian missionaries. In response to such a multitude of circumstances and needs the prayer power of committed world Christians can make a difference. God acts when His people pray.

Chapter Four

Memories of Antiquity

"In the beginning God created the heavens and the earth." (Genesis 1:1) For the Christian this powerful acclamation of the divine creation of the universe forms the foundation for any space or time reference. Whether it is a Christian perspective of geography (where man is in space) or of history (where man is in time), Genesis, chapter one marks the point of departure.

The Chinese have a saying: "To understand a nation, one must understand its memories." Because no nation exists in an historical vacuum, a compassionate understanding of a people today will include the recognition of their past greatness and their appropriate pride in the past.

From a Christian perspective, God is both omnipotent and personal; he has decisively entered into history and changed its course. Although we do not know exactly what His omniscient purposes are in particular events, we can know from a Biblical basis that God's ultimate plan in history is a redemptive plan. He desires that all men everywhere be drawn unto Him. Therefore in surveying Asian history, two conclusions can be made: Asian history does have meaning and ultimately a redemptive plan is taking place in Asia just as it is elsewhere in the world.

India

In few nations of the world are history and religion so intricately bound together as in India. The very name "India" derives from the Sanskrit word *sindhu,* from which word also the river "Indus" is named, as are the religion "Hindu" and the language "Hindi."

The exact origins of Indian civilization are not entirely certain, but a relatively sophisticated civilization lived along the Indus River as early as c.4500 B.C. There, at Mohenjo-Daro and Harappa several developments were laid out in orderly blocks of houses, streets, public baths, and efficient sanitation systems.

However, around 1500 B.C., Indian civilization underwent a drastic change. From the northwest, light skinned Aryans entered the subcontinent and pushed the darker skinned Dravidians to the south. Out of this racial difference, the caste system gradually developed, a system that has brought great hardship and discord to India for hundreds of years.

Soon the caste system became based upon occupation and determined a person's position in society. Although originally four castes existed, today that number exceeds 3,000 castes and subcastes in India. The four castes from which the others have derived are: the *Brahmins,* who were the priestly class; the *Kshatriyas,* who were the warriors; the *Vaisyas,* who were merchants or landowners; and the *Sudras,* who were laborers and peasants. Beneath these castes were the "outcastes," the *pariahs,* whose position was so low that they were considered untouchables. To be touched by an untouchable or even to have the shadow of an untouchable fall across one's path was considered ceremonially unclean. Many centuries later, Mahatma Gandhi, who worked to eliminate untouchability, would call them *Harijans,* "Children of God."

Within the castes, many subcastes or *jatis* developed which governed marriage, housing, religious observances, and occupations. Although the 1950 constitution of India abolished untouchability, the untouchable discrimination persists today as does the entire complicated caste system.

Following the Aryan invasion, the subsequent history of India for almost 3,000 years was marked by repeated invasions by outside forces. Although Alexander the Great invaded northern India in 326 B.C., Greek rule was never fully imposed upon the subcontinent. The invasion resulted in a cross-pollination of East and West that left an enduring mark on both civilizations. In 270 B.C. India was taken over by Mauryan rulers who expanded their authority across northern India, introducing an era characterized by a strong central government with a far-flung bureaucracy, a huge army, and an elaborate network of spies. The Mauryan Empire produced Asoka, one of the ancient world's greatest figures. A multi-talented ruler, Asoka converted to Buddhism and initiated a period of peace and prosperity in India.

However, it was the Gupta Empire (320-535 A.D.) which brought about a true golden age in India. During this two hundred year era of peace and prosperity, India returned to Hinduism. Music, dance, drama, science, and mathematics reached remarkable heights. Many of the tourist sites of contemporary India date back to the Gupta period.

During the eighth century a violent confrontation took place between Hindus and invading Muslims known as Moguls, an event that sowed seeds of bitterness and strife that still exist 1,200 years later. From the 1200's to the 1500's the Muslims competed for power in India until the Moguls emerged triumphant in the mid 1500's. With their impressive capitals at Delhi and Agra, the Moguls established an efficient government that reached its zenith under the magnificent ruler Akbar. Much later, when the British ruled India, they were to look back to Akbar for a model of efficient government.

Perhaps one of the most distinguishing characteristics of Mogul rule was the introduction of a graceful form of architecture in palaces, mosques, and tombs. The breathtakingly beautiful Taj Mahal at Agra is the most celebrated example. Built by the Mogul Emperor Shah Jahan as a tomb for one of his wives, the shimmering Taj represents the apex of symmetry and ornate elegance of Mogul architecture. However, the Mogul empire fell apart under the intolerant rule of Shah Jahan's son, Aurangzeb, thus paving the way for European power to take control of India.

In the European search for overseas wealth, the Portuguese explorer Vasco da Gama touched India in 1498. Subsequently, Dutch, British, and French explorers also made claims along the Indian coast. But it was the British who extended their rule inland after Queen Elizabeth I chartered the British East India Company in 1600.

The coming of the British was a watershed event not just to India but to all of Asia, for it signalled the beginning of the colonial era in Asia—an era which did not end until after World War II. Ancient civilizations, including India, now came face to face with an intruding power for which they were unprepared. Asia was forever changed.

By 1857, after successfully quelling an Indian mutiny, the British Crown took over the rule of all of India. From the viceroy at the top on down to the level of the district commissioner, a well-run bureaucracy reached to the village level in a system reminiscent of Mogul days. What was in it for the British? India supplied cotton, tea and other raw materials for manufacturing. In exchange, the British established schools, built hospitals, instituted a judicial system, introduced the English language, and laid down a vast railroad network.

But the colonial rulers made the mistake of not including Indians in positions of influence and leadership, a mistake which fostered Indian nationalism and unrest by the arrival of the twentieth century. All that was needed was an Indian national leader, a position that was filled by Mohandas K. Gandhi. From the 1920's to 1948, the Mahatma ("great soul") guided the Indians through a non-violent campaign of passive resistance and civil disobedience.

Wisely recognizing that the time had come for withdrawal, the British finally granted independence to India and a newly-created Pakistan on August 15,1947.

The newborn yet antiquated India now became the responsibility of Prime Minister Jawaharlal Nehru. The fact that the nation hung together during the first few years is a tribute to Nehru's personal appeal and wise leadership. Although western-educated and a committed internationalist, Nehru was nevertheless able to inspire Indians at the most basic village level. Following Nehru's death in 1964, India's search for a new leader led in 1966 to Indira Gandhi, Nehru's daughter. Her policies and untimely death contributed to the contemporary issues of India to be discussed in a subsequent chapter.

China

The sense of antiquity in Chinese history is almost impossible for the Westerner to grasp. Whereas European or New World history is measured in centuries, Chinese history is measured in millenia. Wave after wave of momentous events seemed to envelop the great mass of Chinese people, rendering them almost helpless to control their own destiny.

Undoubtedly one of the unique features of Chinese history was the traditional Chinese world view. The Chinese viewed time as a circle, without beginning or end, whereas Westerners traditionally have held to a linear view of history with a sense of a definite beginning and ending. Furthermore, the Chinese concept of the universe was something akin to an inverted bowl with the heavens above and the earth below. At the center of the universe was China, the "Middle Kingdom" (*Chungkou*). To the Chinese, the rest of the inhabitants of the earth, beneath them, were barbarians who had little to offer that the Chinese could possibly want.

From an early farming civilization located along the Huang Ho (Yellow River), a system of dynastic rule emerged, a system that would bring twenty-four dynasties into power in China. Probably the first dynasty was the Shang (c.1850-1100 B.C.) in which the use of bronze in advanced forms is evident. More importantly, an ideographic system of writing on bones was developed which created the foundation for the Chinese written language, a complicated system of pictographs and symbols that now numbers well over 40,000 characters.

However, it was the Chou Dynasty (1000-221 B.C.) that took form in the truly traditional dynastic sense. This was the great age of ancient philosophy which produced such scholars as Confucius and Lao Tzu, founders of Confucianism and Taoism. From the Confucian foundation, Chinese society developed into a highly traditional, stratified culture which changed little over the centuries. The masses of people were landless peasants locked into a ceaseless struggle for existence against nature.

Power rested in the hands of the landed gentry who gained their positions of influence by passing the rigorous Confucian examinations, thus admitting them into the scholarly class. They set the tone of public life and perpetuated the values by which all Chinese were expected to live. Filial piety, veneration of old age, and strong family ties became hallmarks of Confucian society.

Not only was Confucianism developed during the Chou Dynasty, but the Great Wall was also begun. When finally completed some 400 years later, this imposing marvel stretched 1,500 miles through mountainous terrain. Built to keep out invaders, the Great Wall would provide man with one of the wonders of the ancient world, be tramped upon by tourists from all over the world, and enjoy the distinction of being the only made-made object observable from outer space.

Actually China was not a unified state until the Ch'in Dynasty (221-206 B.C.), from which the very name "China" is derived. Although short-lived, the Ch'in Dynasty was a most eventful period under one ruler, now using the name "emperor," Ch'in Shi Huang-ti. Construction of the Great Wall continued, but Confucian scholars were persecuted in bloody encounters. The emperor ordered construction of a massive tomb for himself which has recently provided archaeologists with an immense discovery that well may be one of the greatest archaeological discoveries in history. Located near Xian, the tomb holds nearly 6,000 terra-cotta clay soldiers, some on horseback, each one different from the other in facial features. The emperor's tomb, yet to be excavated, is expected to hold a huge treasure of ancient Chinese wealth.

However, it was the Han Dynasty (202 B.C.-220 A.D.) which provided China with the first of several glorious eras. At the same time, more than 3,000 miles away, in a place called Palestine, the Savior of the world was walking on earth. During this period of strong dynastic rule, the Great Wall was finished at last, a calendar introduced and eclipses accurately predicted. A primitive, yet reasonably accurate, seismograph was developed to measure earthquakes. Caravans along the Silk Road appeared more frequently as the Han Dynasty boosted China's silk trade with the Mediterranean world.

In philosophy and religion, the Han Dynasty introduced long-lasting changes. The Confucian Classics were revered as Confucianism became the philosophical basis for governing. From India came the new and appealing religious force of Buddhism brought by missionaries during the first century A.D. Buddhism in China underwent gradual changes over the centuries, leaving a particularly profound mark on Chinese art. In China, Buddhism developed into a meditative sect called "Chan," which later spread to Japan as "Zen"

The end of the Han Dynasty was characterized by a gradual, disorderly disintegration of Chinese society. Although other dynasties rose and fell during the period, China did not see the flowering of another glorious age until the T'ang Dynasty (623-907 A.D.). A commentary on the longevity and antiquity of China is that its history has seen more than one Golden Age. Certainly the T'ang

Dynasty can be seen as such an era.

When Westerners invoke a mental image of "ancient China," in all likelihood they are thinking of the T'ang Dynasty. Great, colorfully decorated temples and multi-storied pagodas were constructed. Poetry flourished under the influence of Buddhist inspiration and Taoist mysticism. Writing and calligraphy reached such artistic proportions as those expressed in *The Diamond Sutra,* a sixteen foot long "book" which is one of China's national art treasures. Clay pottery was developed into true porcelain, so beautiful and translucent that it was simply called "china." This new development set the standard for porcelains thereafter.

But internal political weaknesses brought about the gradual decline of the T'ang Dynasty. An elaborate, luxurious and carefully ordered court system broke down under the weight of palace intrigues and power struggles. Meanwhile, the impoverished condition of the mass of the Chinese population, the peasantry, continued unabated.

The recurrent theme of the rise and fall of Chinese dynasties continued. Like the T'ang Dynasty, the Sung Dynasty (907-1279) was also a period of intellectual and artistic progress. Wood block printing allowed a wider distribution of literature. Beautiful landscape paintings reflected renewed interest in the meditative study of nature. The delicate Sung porcelains (often greens and blues) are still collectors' items today.

However, the predictable dynastic course of Chinese history was suddenly interrupted in 1279 by the invasion of the Mongols under Genghis and Kublai Khan, who established the largest empire in Asian history. Although they succeeded in imposing themselves over China by the sword, they failed to make accommodations for the power of Chinese culture. Chinese culture was simply too pervasive a force for these nomadic, illiterate intruders. Although their open trade routes allowed contact with Europe (including the famous visit by Marco Polo), the Mongols were expelled by a powerful new Chinese

Dynasty.

The Ming Dynasty (1368-1644) endured the longest of any of the many Chinese dynasties. The capital was moved to Peking where the vast Forbidden City was constructed to house the extensive, luxurious court. Neighboring Asian countries were forced to pay tribute to Ming China in two ways. First, tribute nations had to send valuable products and goods to China. Second, and of equal or even greater importance, ambassadors from tribute countries had to prostrate themselves before the emperor in the famous ritual known as the *kowtow*. In exchange, the foreign relations of the Far East were stabilized and peace maintained. Artistically, the Ming Dynasty produced little that was original with the exception of its extraordinary architectural designs, particularly in Peking, and its exquisite blue and white porcelains.

The last of the Chinese dynastic cycle was the Ch'ing or Manchu Dynasty (1644-1911). This was the great age of empire building during which China reached its present size. Although explosive growth in population occurred during Manchu China, the amount of land subject to taxation decreased because ruling officials who owned land were exempted from taxes.

As a result, the burden of taxation on the peasantry increased to oppressive proportions, a fact that in turn led to seriously disruptive peasant rebellions. The most famous of these peasant disorders was the T'aiping Rebellion (1850-1864) in which as many as 25,000,000 may have lost their lives. Peasants, who comprised the bulk of the Chinese population, lived lives of misery and hardship characterized by dehumanizing conditions and unbending traditions.

The Manchu rulers were instilled with a sense of superiority maintained by a rigidly traditional Confucian-based society. Inscribed over the emperor's throne in the Forbidden City were the Confucian virtues—"balanced, upright, benevolent, and harmonious"—as a reminder of the qualities that would sustain a properly ordered nation. The

Confucian exam became the rite of passage into the civil service, the locus of prestige, wealth, and power. Ensconsed securely atop an unchanging society, the Manchu rulers assumed China would never change. But China was about to encounter a force that would jar the great nation out of its lethargy.

Although the Chinese had shown little interest in the outside world, Europeans were very much interested in China. Begun by the Portuguese in 1514, coastal trade allured British, French, German, and, eventually, Americans. The lucrative Canton trade was largely controlled by the British, who exchanged opium for tea. When the Chinese government tried to cut off the destructive opium trade, the attempt resulted in the Opium War (1840-42) between Great Britain and China. Superior British military power brought quick victory culminating in the Treaty of Nanking in 1842 which ceded Hong Kong (in "perpetuity") to the British. Subsequent treaties gave access to other Chinese ports to traders and interior regions to missionaries. Thus a military defeat for China ultimately resulted in the missionary thrust of the late nineteenth and twentieth centuries.

The Western encroachment signalled the death knell for the Manchu Dynasty. In 1900 the Boxer Rebellion represented a last gasp against Western power as the "Boxers," a mystical Chinese sect, attacked missionaries. Western powers united in rescuing the besieged missionaries in Peking and thus dealt a final blow to the weakened dynasty. A system of rule that had prevailed over 3,500 years ended abruptly in 1912 when China was declared a republic. The new president was Sun Yat-sen, Western-educated and a Christian.

China, the antiquated giant, now embarked on a new and treacherous course which would spawn decades of turmoil as Sun's search to establish nationalist foundations for his giant nation ended with his untimely death in 1925, just four years after the founding of the Chinese communist party in Shanghai. The decade from 1927 to 1937 was one of enormous upheaval and impoverishment in China as the

Nationalists (*Koumintang*,) led by Sun's successor Chiang Kai-shek, and the Communists led by Mao Tse-tung, competed for control of China in a bloody civil war.

The rise of communism in China emerged as one of the most momentous events of the twentieth century and is a topic which has not yet been exhausted by historians. Most of the Communists themselves came from rural areas and successfully captured the hearts and minds of China's huge peasantry, seen by Mao as the revolutionary vanguard.

However, after 1937, the Chinese were fighting both a revolution from within and a national war of resistance against the Japanese who had invaded Manchuria. Although the communists and Nationalists presented a united front in the fight against the Japanese, the Communists were also making inroads in the Chinese countryside. As expected, when World War II ended, civil war broke out between 1,000,000 Communist soldiers and the 3,000,000 Nationalist soldiers, now aided by the U.S. Finally, following loss after loss, the Nationalists under Chiang surrendered in January of 1949 and fled to the island of Formosa.

The announcement of the establishment of the People's Republic of China on October 1, 1949, once more changed the order of affairs in Asia. The world's most populous nation was now communist. The daunting task facing the new rulers was to restructure the highly traditional, rigid Chinese society into a socialist nation. In the decade of the 1950's, China underwent a revolutionary change from the highest echelons of government to the lowest village level. Mao once said "...a revolution is not a dinner party." and indeed what took place in China did so at great human cost.

In order to restructure Chinese society into a socialist and classless society, the strategy was to turn one class against another. Mass organizations were founded to order every facet of people's lives while mass movements were designed to promote government ends. Through confessions, accusations and self-criticism sessions, thought reform, designed to root out pre-communist thinking, was carried out. Some 300,000,000 peasants received land that was placed in communes owned and operated by the state. Perhaps one of the most radical changes was raising the legal status of women to one of equality with men. The role of women drastically changed in a nation where once the word for woman also meant slave.

But for Christians, the changes forced great personal choices when Christians were encouraged to renounce not only their faith but one another. Even though the 1954 constitution guaranteed freedom of religion, Western missionaries were forced to leave and Chinese Christians were persecuted. Although statistics for 1949 are difficult to obtain, estimates suggest some 5,000,000 Chinese were Christians when the Communists took over. Beginning in the 1950's, the Christians were either forced underground or they made accommodations with the government and compromised their faith. (see ch.10)

Undoubtedly the period of greatest upheaval in post-1949 China was the so-called Great Proletarian Cultural Revolution (1966-1976). During those ten lost years, the government tried to wipe out any vestiges of "old China." The entire nation seemed to go berserk when millions of young people known as Red Guards were released to carry out nationwide purges of anyone suspected of opposing the Maoist ideology. Schools were closed, homes ransacked, intellectuals persecuted, city workers sent to the countryside, and party officials purged. Christians endured immense persecution. Suspicion and hatred permeated the society. Finally, the People's Liberation Army was called out to restore order. With the death of Mao in September of 1976 and the arrest of the notorious "Gang of Four" (including Mao's widow), the exhausted country slowly embarked on a new course.

Since the normalization of relations with the West in 1979, China has opened its doors to the modern world to an unprecedented degree. Under the ambitious and pragmatic leadership of the octogenarian Vice Premier Deng Xiaoping, the one billion people of China are attempting to make up for decades of lost time. A new incentive system which encourages private initiative has had surprising results in increased production, although private enterprise in China is still a minor force.

Nevertheless, the future of China is difficult to predict. Deng has reportedly made efforts to prepare for his retirement and has attempted, with some success, to place officials who hold his ideological viewpoint into positions of influence. Whether or not Deng's reforms will be permanent or whether hard-line Maoists can regain power remains to be seen. For Christians, the field in China is ripe for harvest. The church in China is one of the most dynamic and fastest growing anywhere in the world. (see ch.10)

Korea

The history of Korea ("Chosen") has been something of an extension of Chinese history. Its early inhabitants had moved from Manchuria down into the peninsula from which point they eventually crossed over to Japan. By the third century B.C., the first true Korean state developed as a separate entity. However, the Han emperor, Wu, annexed the area to China in the first century B.C. Although certain Korean traditions continued, essentially Korean history is a history of Chinese dominence.

Even during a period known in Korea as the Three Kingdoms, when Korean strength was asserted, Korea served as a cultural bridge conveying Chinese culture to Japan. The Japanese borrowed ideas in government, art, literature, and Buddhism from China via Korea. During the Silla period of Korean history (670-935), a period of Korean unification, the borrowing of Chinese culture continued. The last strong epoch in Korean history was the Koryo period, which lasted until 1392.

By the fourteenth century Korea had become a

tributary state of China with continued close cultural ties to China, particularly those pertaining to Confucianism. The first European contact occurred in 1593 when a Spanish Jesuit reached Korean shores. A full Jesuit mission from Peking soon arrived and claimed some 9,000 converts by 1839. In that year many Christian converts and three priests were put to death while others endured persecution. By 1866, the entire Christian community of 16,000 had been wiped out.

Despite Chinese influence over Korea, the nation began to gain international status by opening its doors through trade treaties with Japan (1876) and the United States (1882). By the end of the century, both Chinese and Japanese interest in dominating Korea had taken on new dimensions. The Japanese saw Korea as a "dagger aimed at the heart of Japan." The brief Sino-Japanese War broke out in 1894 and, much to the world's surprise, Japan defeated China. Japan's victory marked a new era in Asian politics when Japan ascended as a major power. From China, Japan demanded the independence of Korea, then pronounced it a Japanese protectorate in 1905 until it was annexed outright in 1910.

Until the end of World War II, Korea suffered under prolonged Japanese rule during which Japanese culture was forced upon the Koreans. Resentment against the Japanese ran deep. The collapse of Japan's power over Korea after World War II was followed by Russian and American military postwar occupation, divided at the 38th Parallel.

When negotiations on relations between the two zones reached an impasse, the problem was taken to the newly created United Nations. Part of the problem was that industry and mining were concentrated in the north while the south was largely agricultural. A Korean communist faction in the north was given encouragement by Stalinist Russia while America was trying to supervise the establishment of democratic institutions in the south. United Nations-authorized elections in 1948 produced the

Republic of Korea in the south under the presidency of Singman Rhee. A communist government was established in the north under Prime Minister Kim Il-song.

There matters stood when North Korean armies suddenly struck across the 38th Parallel on June 25,1950. During a boycott of UN activities by the Soviet Union, a resolution was approved sending a multi-national force to Korea. The Korean War had begun, a war that ended in a cease-fire in 1953 and which brought long-term suffering to the Korean people. Negotiations still continue across the table at the Demilitarized Zone, a situation that always looms in the background of contemporary Korean issues. (see ch.10)

Chapter Five

Of Samurai and Missionaries

Japan

Of all the nations of Asia, Japan has a particularly unique and fascinating history, one which has produced a people who say with meaningful distinctiveness, "We are the Japanese." What uniquely characterizes Japanese history is its gradual, uninterrupted progression, interspersed with long periods of isolation. Japan is, foremost, an island country (*shimaguni*). That fact results in a strong sense of nationality among the Japanese and a defined awareness of homogeneity. Although its position on the outer edge of Chinese civilization allowed the absorption of considerable Chinese influence, Japan remained separated.

The Japanese creation legend embodies the concept of a nation divinely created. Two important deities, Izanagi (male) and Izanami (female) thrust a spear into the waters to create the first of the Japanese islands with the others to follow. Among the deities, the Sun Goddess, Amaterasu Omikami, became the progenitor of a long line of emperors stretching from Jimmu Tenno to Hirohito.

Beyond this concept of divine creation, the Japanese archipelago appears to have been populated first by the Jomon (c.4,500 B.C.), a pottery-making people, although some evidence of a paleolithic settlement has been unearthed. Later, an aboriginal Ainu people settled on the north island of Hokkaido in about 3,500 B.C. But the first significant settlement of population was composed of the Yoyoi people, who perhaps migrated from the Korean peninsula. Appearing about 300 B.C., the Yoyoi were agriculturalists who brought with them horses and cattle. Throughout Japanese history and even in the present, farmers have played a very important role.

As early as this period of Japanese history, several factors developed that still play a role in modern Japanese society and which should be kept in mind by Christians sharing the Gospel. The first was the increasing importance placed on the *uji* or clan (anyone related by blood). Each *uji* had its own chiefs and its own shrines. The strong sense of "belonging" and of group identification had its origins before the time of Christ but continues today. Whether it is the firm or company for which one works, a school, a university, woman's association, or hobby group to which one belongs, the important thing is that one is "within" (*uchi*). For a Japanese, to become a Christian may mean breaking ties with one's group, not an easy thing to do.

The second historical factor which can be seen at a very early stage in Japanese history and which also should be kept in mind in sharing the Gospel is the development of Shintoism, the "Way of the Gods." Centering around the worship of *kami* or local spiritual forces, Shintoism is a distinctively Japanese religion (see ch.6) which evolved into the official state religion. Its early high priests were also temporal rulers.

Another important factor in Japanese history was the spread of Chinese influence. In the seventh century A.D., Japan embraced Chinese civilization enthusiastically. Chinese Buddhist influence had already made its way into the royal court during the previous century. By 645 A.D., the Japanese embarked on a conscious effort to massively borrow from Chinese culture on a scale unique to its own history. At a time when European culture was stagnating,

Japanese culture began to flourish.

Among the Chinese cultural characteristics adopted by the Japanese was that of a powerful monarchy. In this case, the Japanese emperor became both the Shintoist religious leader and the secular ruler positioned above a highly centralized state. The capital was first established at Nara and later moved to Kyoto.

Not only did the Japanese adopt the Chinese concept of government, but they also borrowed Chinese Confucian philosophy with its emphasis on filial piety. Japanese art and architecture were transformed by the elegant influence of Chinese culture. By the eighth and ninth centuries, Buddhism had spread throughout Japan.

However, despite their substantial borrowing from China, the Japanese managed to maintain their own identity—a characteristic prevalent throughout their history. An attempt by the Chinese in 1281 to invade Japan was thwarted by a divine wind (*kamikaze*) which destroyed a massive fleet carrying 150,000 men. The Japanese sense of identity was also maintained by their distinctive language which they maintained even though they adopted Chinese characters (*kanji*). By the ninth century, the Japanese had developed their own efficient writing system.

By the twelfth century, Japan had taken a new direction due primarily to its geographic isolation. Although they had adopted the Chinese centralized state system, the Japanese had also supported a system of land ownership which led to the development of large tax-free estates. This system evolved into a form of feudalism not unlike that of Europe at the same time. Based on loyalty, a strong warrior class known as the *samurai* developed. Unlike European knights, however, the samurai prided themselves in their artistic pursuits, even to the extent of turning martial activity into art forms. Buddhist influence lent itself to the graceful simplicity of Japanese art and architecture as well as to the fact that many of the samurai preferred the meditative forms of Zen Buddhism.

Although the emperor remained on his throne in

Kyoto, the real power of Japan was in the hands of the most powerful of landed nobles, the *shoguns*, beginning with the Kamakura Shogunate in 1185. For eight centuries Japan remained in unbroken military rule based upon loyalty and family ties. The last of the great shogunates was the Tokugawa which lasted from 1603 to 1868.

The most significant feature about the last shogunate is that Japan embarked upon a 200 year period of seclusion from the rest of the world, a policy known as *sakoku*. The capital was moved to Edo (today's Tokyo) and a long period of peace ensued. The rice economy was concentrated in the hands of feudal barons and administered by a hierarchical system of bureaucratic control. A merchant class developed to help provide the luxury goods demanded by court nobility. But the bulk of the population was a peasantry languishing under a heavy tax burden.

Not only did the Japanese want nothing to do with the outside world during this period of time, but they also persecuted Christians because this religion was seen as an "outside" influence. Christianity had come to Japan via the Jesuits in 1549. The missionaries were accepted and respected, perhaps partially for economic reasons since traders often came into the country alongside missionaries. However, the missionaries were banned during the Tokugawa Shogunate and Japanese Christians were persecuted. Some 3,000 were martyred when they refused to step on metalic images of Jesus Christ placed on the ground for them to desecrate.

But an historic change was about to take place in Japan, one which had already altered Indian and Chinese history; Western powers were knocking on Japan's closed door. In 1853, four tall black ships anchored in Edo Bay. These ships, commanded by Commodore Matthew Perry of the United States, signaled the end of Japan's isolation from the rest of the world. Within a year, the Japanese made the revolutionary decision to open trade with the U.S. and, ultimately, with other Western countries.

Not only did Japan open its doors to the outside world

but the nation also soon rid itself of the feudalistic system. The shogunate was overthrown and imperial rule returned in 1868 in what is known in Japanese history as the Meiji Restoration. The new emperor became the rallying point for reform-minded leaders. Japan embarked on a massive reform program aimed at catching up with the rest of the world.

The Japanese were quick learners. In four decades they made amazing progress in modernization. The government encouraged shipbuilding and the growth of a cotton textile industry. Port facilities and railroads were built and telegraph and postal systems established. The Japanese embarked on a deliberate program of borrowing foreign ideas. From the Americans came ideas about education, from the Germans came principles of the military and science, from the French came concepts of government and law, from the British came naval procedures. A constitution and multi-party political system were instituted.

By the time of World War I, Japan had developed into a world power to be reckoned with particularly after it defeated Russia in 1905 in a conflict over control of Korea. At the end of World War I, the Versailles Treaty gave Japan some of Germany's former colonies in the Pacific. Not only was Japan now involved in imperialism, but it also moved toward militarism in the 1920's and 1930's.

A combination of economic disparity between rural and urban areas, of unfulfilled expectations of a young educated class, and of government corruption produced a militaristic reaction. Added to these internal problems was the fear that Japan's economy was being stifled by Western powers. The answer seemed to lay in military expansion into the Asian continent.

Subsequently, in 1931, Manchuria was overrun by Japanese soldiers. Gradual Japanese extension into other areas of China led to full-scale fighting in July of 1937. Soon, combined with the war in Europe, World War II had erupted. Japan's announced intention was the establishment of a Greater East Asia Co-Prosperity Sphere, an arrangement designed to supply Japan's economy with raw materials.

To accomplish that goal, Japanese military offenses were launched between 1941 and 1945 against Pearl Harbor in Hawaii, French Indochina, Thailand, Hong Kong, the Malay Peninsula, Singapore, Burma, the Philippines, Indonesia, the Solomon Islands, New Guinea, and numerous smaller islands of the South Pacific. Not until 1942, at Midway Island, did Japanese victories turn to defeats. The last three years of the war marked a hard-fought retreat culminating in the dropping of the first atomic bombs on the industrial sites of Hiroshima (August 6,1945) and Nagasaki (August 9, 1945).

When one looks at the dynamic country Japan is today, it is hard to envision what it was like in 1945. All of its major cities, except Kyoto, were destroyed, industry was at a standstill, and agricultural production had fallen dramatically. Some 700,000 civilians were among the war dead in addition to the military casualties. Worse still was the damage to the Japanese psyche; the populace, so long responding with such tremendous will power, was spiritually drained. A national sense of betrayal at the hands of the military leaders prevailed.

Such feelings opened the Japanese not only to the American-led occupation forces, but also to the new ideas the forces introduced. Under the command of Gen. Douglas MacArthur, a new Japan was set in motion. First, Japan was demilitarized and a new constitution written to establish a democracy in which the emperor remained powerless but acted as a figurehead. Furthermore, nine years of compulsory education were required, a ruling eventually producing a highly literate nation in which a high premium is placed on academic achievement. Finally, the redistribution of farm land to former tenants could be counted among the most important of the economic reforms.

The other significant economic reform in postwar

Japan was the breakup of the *zaibatsu,* the giant industrial conglomerates that had long been in family ownerships. Labor unions were allowed to form in most major industries. Moreover, postwar policies of the Japanese government have been highly favorable to capital investment. Ironically, wartime devastation provided an unexpected benefit when Japan's newly-built industrial facilities became among the world's most modern and efficient.

A postscript of interest to Christians should be added. Among the suggestions of Gen. Douglas MacArthur as commander of the Japanese occupational forces was to invite missionaries into Japan. He believed that Japan existed in a spiritual vacuum and therefore open to conversion to Christianity, a religion he linked with democracy. By 1950 over a thousand missionaries responded to MacArthur's invitation, many involved in a project to disseminate 10,000,000 Bibles throughout Japan. But Christianity made little headway in postwar Japan partially because of the deeply ingrained beliefs in Shintoism and Buddhism and partially because Christianity was identified with the Occupation and with its soldiers whose behavior was often an affront to the Japanese.

Southeast Asia

The early history of Southeast Asia (a term first used during World War II) is an amalgam which reflects the peninsular geography of the area. From the valleys of China and Tibet the early inhabitants made their way down the peninsula and across to the island archipelagos. Principal ethnic groups included Malays, Chams on the east coast, Khmers and Mons of present-day Burma and Thailand. As early as 500 B.C. the Malays and Indonesians had made their way to the Philippines. Animistic in their religion, these farming people instituted a wet-rice agriculture still widely practiced today.

Because Southeast Asia's location lies on the water

route between India and China, trading settlements were
established, particularly by Indians. Thus a pattern of
adapting Indian ideas, albeit in differing forms, shaped the
early history of Southeast Asia. Several powerful kingdoms
were established, most notably the Funan at the tip of
Vietnam, Srivijaya on the Strait of Malacca and Khmer,
the most famous of all. Situated in the fertile lowlands of
the Southeast Asian mainland, the Khmer capital was the
splendid city of Angkor with its numerous ornate temples.
Ironically, those beautiful temples contributed to the
downfall of the Khmer state. So much investment went
into temple building that the Khmer state was weakened
and subsequently captured by neighboring Thai states.

While Indianization characterized much of Southeast
Asia, exceptions to that influence were the Philippines,
which were located off the main India-China trade route,
and Vietnam, which came under Chinese rule in 111 B.C.
and remained so until the tenth century A.D. Meanwhile
the Kingdoms of Laos and of Siam each expanded until the
latter became the strongest of the mainland areas by the
eighteenth century.

However, as was true in the histories of other Asian
regions, outside powers changed the course of Southeast
Asian history. The new religion of Islam and the arrival of
European traders exerted powerful forces. From India, Islamic traders brought their religion to Sumatra, Malaya,
Java and eventually all the way to the Philippines. By the
fifteenth and sixteenth centuries, Islam had become the
dominant force that not only could be used to oppose the
Hindu states but could also provide a common bond used
to oppose Christian European traders.

These European traders traced their origins to the
voyage of Vasco da Gama to India in 1498. From there,
Portuguese traders ventured out in an attempt to control
the spice trade. In 1519, Ferdinand Magellan set out for
the Moluccas, eventually arriving in the Philippines, which
he claimed for Spain.

Soon other European nations, including the Dutch,

British, French, Swedish, and Danish sent trading ships to the area in search of precious raw materials such as rubber, sugar cane, and much desired spices. A colonial pattern quickly evolved. Indonesia became a Dutch colony while England colonized Burma, the Malaysian Peninsula, and northern Borneo. Vietnam, Laos, and Cambodia came under French colonization. The Philippines remained in the hands of the Spanish until 1898 when the United States took over rule after the Spanish-American War. Only Siam (today's Thailand) never fell into the hands of a colonial power.

Colonial rule was not altogether negative in its influence. To an area frequently rent by warfare, the colonial powers brought centuries of relative peace. In each colony, a major city was established, such as Singapore, Rangoon, and Jakarta. Schools, hospitals, improved health standards, and a decrease in infant mortality could be traced directly to colonial rule.

However, two major errors occurred during the course of colonial rule. Because Westerners were interested primarily in taking out raw materials, little manufacturing was established. Moreover, Southeast Asians were given little opportunity to gain experience in self-government. Not surprisingly, a nationalist movement developed by the end of the nineteenth century, beginning in Indonesia.

By the 1930's, the nationalist movement had gained momentum throughout much of Southeast Asia but was interrupted by World War II. Japan needed the raw materials which Southeast Asia offered. By August of 1942, almost all of Southeast Asia was under Japanese control as a result of a string of military victories.

Although the Japanese occupation lasted four years, it set the stage for eventual independence for most of Southeast Asia. The power and prestige of European rule was broken. Furthermore, the Japanese-trained native armies provided the training ground for leaders who would later demand independence. Within twenty-five years of the war's end, most Southeast Asian nations gained their independence. The Philippines won independence in 1946, Burma in 1948, Indonesia in 1950, Malaya in 1957, and Singapore in 1965.

Only Indo-Chinese independence dragged out in excruciating years of warfare which have not yet been wholly resolved. From 1946 to 1954, the French engaged in guerilla warfare with the communists (Vietminh). Vietnam was partitioned in 1954 while Laos and Cambodia were granted independence. The Vietnam War stretched on until 1974 when South Vietnam was united with North Vietnam under communist rule.

This strategic area, for all its dynamic potential, remains a product of its splintered geography and its cultural, ethnic, and political disunity. Almost 75 per cent of its workers are engaged in farming, living in highly traditional patterns. Time and history have exerted little impact on such people whose pattern of existence has been governed not by historical epochs, but by the rhythm of the seasons.

From a Christian perspective, three factors in Southeast Asian history are significant. First is the historic and continuing ethnic variety which presents a multitude of linguistic and cultural challenges. Second is the ever-present difficulty in disseminating the Gospel, due to geographic difficulties ranging from mountainous tropical terrain to scattered islands difficult to reach. Third is the paramount influence of three very strongly developed religious systems, Buddhism, Hinduism, and Islam.

Christian Missions in Asia

An overview of Asian history would be incomplete from a Christian perspective if it did not also include a look at what missions have accomplished in Asia in the last 1,900 years. One can refer to that span of time because it was in approximately 52 A.D. that the Apostle Thomas made his way to India where, after twenty years of sharing truths about the One whom his own eyes had seen and his hands had touched, he was martyred and buried in Madras. From India a small group of Nestorian Christians made their way to Xian, China in 635. There the religion was perceived as anti-thetical to Chinese philosophy and failed to gain a foothold.

Perhaps the most effective of the earliest missionaries was Francis Xavier, a Jesuit, who worked in India from 1541 to 1545 before going eastward to Malacca, going through the Moluccan Islands and on to Japan, where he reported a total of some 40,000 converts in just four years. The Jesuits also persisted in China in the seventeenth century, endearing themselves to the imperial court because of their superior knowledge. Quite possibly there were as many as 300,000 Chinese Christians by the end of the seventeenth century.

But the era of Protestant evangelical missions in Asia can be traced to the remarkable Englishman William Carey (1761-1834). With a heart concerned for the lost of the world, the young Carey gave an impassioned plea for missions with the exhortation, "Expect great things from God, attempt great things for God." His plea planted seeds that produced twelve new Protestant mission societies between 1792 and 1824. With his reluctant wife and four children, Carey arrived in India in 1793 after an arduous five-month journey from England. Incredibly, during his forty years in India, he translated the Bible into 35 languages, started numerous schools and a college, disseminated literature and led a campaign for social reform.

At about the same time, another pioneer Protestant missionary, Adoniram Judson and his courageous wife Nancy, left their Massachusetts home bound for India and eventually for Burma. There Judson translated the Bible into Burmese, was imprisoned for his faith, and labored faithfully at the head of a mission until his death in 1850. The Judson story poignantly illustrates the sacrifice of early missionaries as they endured discouragements, illnesses, long separations from children, and the loss of loved ones.

With its huge size, its rigid society, and its hatred of "foreign devils," China represented the greatest Asian missionary challenge of all. The first Protestant missionary to China was the Scotsman Robert Morrison, who arrived in Canton in 1807. Fluent in Chinese, Morrison translated the Bible. Seven years later he won his first convert, Liang, a courageous young printer who faithfully served the Lord for thirty-four years under great persecution. During Morrison's twenty-five arduous years in China, he could count fewer than a dozen converts. But he had pioneered the most difficult of Asian mission frontiers.

Thereafter, dozens of Protestant missionaries from a variety of mission societies responded to God's call to China, frequently laboring under incredible hardship, often dying in obscurity with little earthly reward for their dedication. But of all the seemingly impossible mission achievements in China, few have approached that of Hudson Taylor. In 1853, at the age of twenty-one, he left his native England for an unknown future in China. He changed to Chinese dress, adopted much of the Chinese lifestyle and set out for the interior. There he wrote a small book, *China's Spiritual Needs and Claims*, which, when read in England, had the magnetic effect of drawing dozens of volunteers to Taylor's new mission, the China Inland Mission. The mission was unique in two ways: there were no missionary salaries, and it was interdenominational. Many of the volunteers were single women, whom Taylor recognized as having a unique ministry among Chinese women.

But Taylor's faithful years in China ended in the shadow of his great personal sadness resulting from the Boxer Rebellion (1900) in which 135 missionaries and 35 missionary children were murdered, most of them from the CIM. Nevertheless, by the time of his death in 1905, Hudson Taylor's China Inland Mission established 849 missions in China and had sent 6,000 missionaries throughout China. A life wholly yielded to the Lord had been vastly multiplied.

With the exception of the China Inland Mission, the results of many of these pioneering efforts may seem small by present standards. There were, however, significant obstacles to early mission activities. First, these missionaries encountered ancient, well-developed civilizations that fostered condescension toward things Western. Second, the early missionaries came face to face with firmly entrenched religions and philosophies such as Hinduism, Buddhism, and Confucianism. Finally, unquestionably Christianity was identified with colonialism, an identity which gave Christianity a negative connotation difficult for missionaries to overcome.

Despite these obstacles, a great deal of credit must go to early Christian missions not only for proclaiming the good news of Jesus Christ, but for alcohol reform, elevation of the status of women, abolition of child marriage, the forbidding of female infanticide, and halting practices such as slave trade, cannibalism, human sacrifices, self-immolation of widows, and foot binding. In addition, schools, hospitals, leper colonies and sanitation facilities were established.

Though these pioneers in Asian missions made mistakes, often with the best of intentions, they labored under hardships that would deter most people today. Many never returned to their homelands and stood sadly by as their loved ones, including small children, succumbed to tropical diseases. They were members of that faith honor roll listed in Hebrews, chapter eleven, "for whom the world was not worthy." Today, the prayers uttered a hundred years ago by these missions pioneers are being answered by a wave of eager young missionaries. The seeds they planted decades ago are at last bearing the fruit of a great Asian harvest.

This Islamic mosque in Hyderabad, India is only one of hundreds of mosques scattered throughout Asia as evidence of the increasing strength of Islam. The style of architecture of nearly all Asian mosques reflects the Arab influence which accompanies Islam.

The polytheistic nature of Hinduism is displayed in the sculptures of this Hindu temple in India. The sculptors have attempted to depict some of the myriads of gods and goddesses of India's major religion.

An early morning scene at Benares (Varanasi), India shows Hindu pilgrims who have come to bathe in the sacred waters of the Ganges River. Considered one of the most sacred sites of India, Benares is also the location of cremation ghats from which ashes of the dead are sprinkled into the river.

(Photo by Robert Lind)

A young boy in Nepal carries a precious bundle of wood on his back. Forests in many areas of Asia are rapidly being denuded as wood is being used in increasing amounts for cooking fuel.

The Shintoist belief in the divine origins of Japan and in the sacred beauty of its landscape combine with the Zen Buddhist emphasis on quiet meditation to produce peaceful parks and gardens such as this one.

(Photo by Robert Lind)

Evidence of changing values can be seen in this provocative movie billboard in Bangkok. Located in a city dotted with Buddhist monasteries, the advertisement suggests values which are a considerable departure from those of the Buddhist Eightfold Path.

Traditional dance remains a major form of art in changing Asia. Classical Indian dance, such as that shown here from northern India, often retells an epic tale from the past.

The extension of the global village includes such sights as fast-food restaurants like these Western franchises located in Tokyo.

In traditional settings throughout Asia, women carry out assigned roles which have changed little over centuries. Here, women in rural India asssist in the harvest.

A national landmark, the huge Kamakura Buddha in Japan is the largest sculpture in the world of a seated Buddha. The Buddha is depicted in the lotus position in a state of nirvana.

Chapter Six

Mother of Religions
and Her Offspring

When God created man (mankind), He made him body, soul, and spirit. Whether or not modern man chooses to recognize it, the spiritual aspect of this triune nature ranks as the most important of the three because it is the spirit in man that cries out to know the Creator. God arranged for that when He "...set eternity in the hearts of men." (Eccles. 3:11) This passage explains why man is inherently "religious," whether his religion be Hinduism, Buddhism, Christianity, or whether that religion perhaps be professional sports, Wall Street finances, or academic intellectualism. A spiritual void inhabits man that must be filled.

Moreover, the pervasive influence of a nation's religion upon its people can be seen in Psalms 115:3-8, a passage describing the gods that are worshipped and ending with the pronouncement "Those who make them will be like them, and so will all who trust in them." This scripture suggests that man becomes like the gods he worships.

Furthermore, the scripture tells us that God has revealed Himself to every nation and people. Psalm 19 assures us that "The heavens declare the glory of God. (v. 1) There is no speech or language where their voice is not heard." (v. 3) Not only has God revealed Himself, but all people everywhere, of any era, have been prepared to receive the gospel.

Yet people have made other spiritual choices. When Jesus Christ made the exclusive claim "I am the Way, the Truth and the Life, no man comes to the Father but by Me." (John 14:6) Hinduism, Confucianism, Taoism, Buddhism, and Shintoism were already firmly established in Asia. Strictly speaking, all five of the world's great religions (Judaism, Hinduism, Buddhism, Christianity, and Islam) are Asian in origin if one considers Israel and Saudi Arabia as geographically part of the Asian continent.

While Christians may justifiably rejoice in the fact that more people have become Christian in the last twenty-five years than in all of previous Christian history, the growth of the religions of Asia represents an extremely formidable challenge. Partially due to high birth rates but also due to very aggressive proselytizing efforts, Islam, Hinduism, and Buddhism have witnessed growth rates which in many areas exceed that of Christianity. Islam is the fastest growing religion in the world and now ranks as the second largest religion in Western Europe.

What need in humankind is it that these religions seek to answer? All people, in whatever primitive or technologically advanced state they might exist, seek answers to three very basic questions. Who am I? Where did I come from? Where am I going? For a Christian, the answer to the question of man's identity is declared in Genesis 1:27, which clearly states that man is created in the image of God. Therein lies his whole human identification and uniqueness. Where did I come from? Genesis 1:1 makes the Christian response in the all encompassing acclamation "In the beginning God created...." Man came from God and God intends that man return to Him. Revelation 21:1-4 reveals the point to which every Christian is going, "Then I saw a new heaven and a new earth...." The revelation of who God is and man's relationship to Him, as found in the Bible, forms the whole basis of the Biblical world view.

From a Biblical standpoint, many religions have asked the "right" questions but have come up with non-Biblical answers. Among all peoples, whatever their religion, are genuine seekers of the truth. These are the seekers of truth throughout the world whom God draws to Himself. Scripture confirms that "You will seek me and find me when you seek me with all your heart." (Jer. 29:13) As a response to this passage, Christians are reminded to "Ask the Lord of the harvest, therefore, to send out workers into His harvest field." (Matt.9:38) Of these truth seekers, many can be found within the world of Hinduism.

Hinduism

If one were to ask a dozen Hindus to explain their religion, the questioner would no doubt hear a dozen differing answers, so wide is its ethereal nature. Hinduism has sometimes been referred to as a "giant sponge" which has managed to absorb and accommodate a host of varying beliefs.

To its adherents, Hinduism is the "Mother of Religions." In few parts of the world are a religion, a nation, and a people so inextricably intertwined as in India. The very names of the nation (India) and its religion (Hinduism) are derived from the same Sanskrit root word. To almost 82 per cent of India's people, to be Indian is to be Hindu and to be Hindu is to be Indian. Furthermore, its force has reached far beyond its own adherents due to its influence upon Buddhism, Jainism, Sikhism and, more recently, in its influence in the Western world through Transcendental Meditation, Hare Krishna, Divine Light Mission, and the New Age Movement.

The origins of Hinduism are somewhat obscure but apparently date back to c. 1500 B.C. to the Vedic period, the time of the Aryan invasion into India. Certain priestly teachings were written in the Vedic scriptures, later combined into the *Upanishads* and the *Mahabharata* (a part of which is the *Bhagavad Gita*). No particular founder or personality is identified with Hinduism.

Unlike Christianity, Hinduism presents gods who combine a mystical merger of the infinite and the finite as well as the impersonal. This concept contrasts with the Biblical characterization of God as both infinite and personal. But perhaps the most confusing aspect of Hinduism to the Western inquirer is that of being simultaneously monotheistic and polytheistic. Running through Hindu thought is the thread of dualism, that is, of unity within diversity.

To a Hindu, there is one god, Brahman, the Absolute, who is manifested in an elaborate pantheon of 330 million gods and goddesses. Hindu temple sculpture is often an incredible array of myriads of gods and goddesses. Of these, three are most often worshipped: Brahma, the creator; Vishnu, the preserver; and Shiva, the destroyer. Thus, creation, preservation, and destruction work as simultaneous forces in the universe.

As is true of most religions of Asia, Hinduism in its most popular form, particularly at the most basic village level, reveals a religion influenced by a variety of forces. Animism, magic, exorcism, and centuries-old superstitions are far more commonplace than is a definable theology based on Vedic scriptures. In its popular form, individuals worship a favorite god or goddess and hope for blessing, prosperity, and peace.

However, an attempt to simplify Hinduism, would suggest that at its basis rest three suppositions: the Law of Karma, the concept of reincarnation, and the practice of a caste system. Each suggests the other two. The Law of Karma is the universal law of cause and effect, that whatever happens in this life was predetermined by something from a previous life. The result is reincarnation in which one's present being is only one existence in a long line of previous and future existences. Because a believer's reincarnated status is dependent upon his karma, there is no such thing as equality. Hence the caste system incorporates as an acceptable part of Hinduism. Simply put, a Hindu's caste affiliation was predetermined in a previous life from which he was reincarnated.

In a broad sense, Hinduism rests on the proposition that a human being can have whatever he wants. He can indulge in worldly passions and the pursuit of pleasure because inevitably the time will arrive, during one of his progressive incarnations, when a person will reach a point of renunciation based upon disillusionment. "What do I really want?" will be his philosophical question, motivated by his desire to free himself from the bondage of the world. What man truly wants, suggests Hinduism, is infinite being (to live forever), infinite knowledge (to know mysteries of the universe), and infinite joy (to satisfy the senses).

In other words, he wants to be like God because these are the accepted god-like qualities. Hindus believe that man already has within him this quality of being like God because every person is part of God and God lives in every person. This "eternal within" must simply be realized. Known as "monism," this concept suggests that there is no difference between God and man; the two are one. The created and the Creator are united.

From a Christian perspective, this concept is crucial to understanding the differences between Hinduism with its offshoots (such as the New Age Movement) and Christianity. By way of background, consider the Biblical account of the trees in the Garden of Eden. In Genesis 2:9, we are told that the trees offered those things which were pleasing to the eye and to the palate (infinite joy), a knowledge of good and evil (infinite knowledge), and life (infinite life).

Interestingly, those attributes for which Hindus have searched for centuries are no different from those desires which tempted man in the beginning. The key restriction in the Garden of Eden was that man must not eat from the tree of knowledge of good and evil because doing so would make him like God. The same suggestion made by the Tempter in Genesis 3:5 "...and you will be like God" lies at the basis of Hinduism. This is extremely important for the Christian to remember when trying to understand Hinduism and its offshoots.

These religions espouse that you already have God within you; you can be god-like. This monistic concept that God is in us and we are God, therefore all are really one, sadly eliminates one of the most beautiful aspects of both man and God as explained in the Bible. Appearing throughout the Bible is the incredible suggestion that man and God are capable of cultivating a relationship. To consider that a human being can have an intimate relationship with the majestic Creator of the universe is an astounding, life-changing concept. But if man and God are one, there can be no relationship between them since a relationship, by its very definition, requires at least two persons. Thus monism robs man of the most meaningful purpose for which he was created—-relationship with the living God.

To a Hindu, this path to oneness with the Absolute (Brahman) is the journey to *moksha* in which the traveler is at last released from the bondages of this life. Such a state can best be reached through the path of *yoga*, the discipline that leads to union with the Absolute. One can choose *jnana yoga* (seeking God intellectually), *karma yoga* (seeking God through works), *bhakti yoga* (seeking God through devotion), or *raja yoga* (seeking God through body and mind control). These four paths form the structure around which Hindu rituals are based whether they be the daily practices such as *puja* or the numerous holiday observances.

In view of all this, what should the Christian response be? Certain common ground already exists between a Hindu and a Christian. The Hindu is a deeply religious person having a reverence for sacred scriptures and a respect for a holy life. He already harbors a strong belief in the existence of God. Therefore the truths of the Gospel must be given both with clarity and respect, building upon the common aspects already existing between Christianity and Hinduism.

A definite Biblical response exists for the three presuppositions of Hinduism. The Law of Karma enslaves a human being to a wheel of existence from which there is no escape. The consequent sense of fatalism breeds hope-lessness and resignation. Therefore, to the Hindu, the Christian can bring a message of hope and freedom through Jesus Christ who declared, "...if the Son sets you free, you will be free indeed." (John 8:36) Or, to put it in Hindu terms, the message of the Gospel is that Jesus took upon Himself "our karma" so that we might inherit "His karma."

In response to the whole concept of reincarnation, the Bible proclaims in Hebrews 9:27 that "...man is destined to die once, and after that to face judgment." Simply stated, there is virtually no Biblical foundation in either the Old or New Testaments for the belief in reincarnation. Moreover, reincarnation deprives a human being of the uniqueness of his existence, a uniqueness which comes from having been created in the image of God.

Finally, the Christian response to the Hindu concept of the caste system can be found in the proclamation of Christian liberty and equality of Galatians 3:26-28. "You are all sons of God through faith in Christ Jesus, for all of you who were baptized into Christ have clothed yourselves in Christ. There is neither Jew nor Greek, slave nor free, male nor female, for you are all one in Christ." God's design is that in Christ all are equal.

Because the Hindu is searching for peace and an escape from the fear of the future, the passage in Hebrews 2:15 can be a message of great hope to the Hindu. Christ's sacrifice was to break the power of death "...and free those who all their lives were held in slavery by their fear of death." The Christian message for the Hindu, given in love, is one of freedom, liberation, hope, and of relation-ship with a living and personal God.

Buddhism

The visitor to Bangkok may stand in awe at the gleaming gold temples with their intricate roof lines. There, the huge, reclining Buddha has become one of Thailand's major tourist attractions and is a great national treasure. The visitor to Kamakura, Japan may gaze in astonishment at the impressive size of the Kamakura Buddha, located in an open courtyard and sublimely seated in the lotus position. In passing countless Buddhist temples and small shrines, the Christian may be reminded of the words of the Psalmist, "But their idols are silver and gold, made by the hands of men. They have mouths, but cannot speak, eyes, but they cannot see; they have ears, but cannot hear, noses, but they cannot smell; they have hands, but cannot feel, feet, but they cannot walk; nor can they utter a sound with their throats. Those who make them will be like them, and so will all who trust in them." (Psalm 115:3-8)

Unlike Hinduism, Buddhism was founded by a particular person, Siddhartha Gautama (560-480 B.C.). Most of the temple and shrine statuary is either of this man—the Buddha—or of a Bodhisattva (one who guides others to enlightenment). Buddhism has sometimes been referred to as a reform of Hinduism because its origins were within Hinduism itself.

According to Buddhist tradition, Gautama was an Indian prince who was married and had a son. At the time of Gautama's birth, legend says that his father was told by a Hindu holy man that this extraordinary child would grow up to be either a political figure or a religious leader. Not wanting the latter, Gautama's father ordered the palace servants to isolate the prince from the realities of Indian life.

One day, however, when Gautama was in his early twenties, he somehow left the palace and, in wandering about, saw what Buddhist tradition considers The Four Passing Sights. Even today, one need not go far in India to see what Gautama saw: old age, sickness, and death. He wondered if there might be a place where these realities of the human condition no longer exist. Then he saw a saddhu, a holy man, and thought perhaps such a disciplined life might hold the answer.

Thus it was that Gautama, at the age of twenty-nine,

left his wife and son in the middle of the night and began his lifelong search for spiritual enlightenment. He rejected the caste system and its rigid inequality. Rather, he sought The Middle Way, away from the ritualism and mysticism of Hinduism, and at the same time away from the indulgent pleasures of his former princely life. In his search, he went through phases of extremism in fasting and of inflicting severe punishment upon his body, finally trying meditation. Buddhist tradition suggests that Gautama finally arrived in Benares (Varanasi) where he meditated under a Bo tree for forty days and nights enduring great opposition from evil forces.

At last enlightenment came while the earth shook and lotus blossoms rained from heaven. Henceforth, he would be the Buddha, the "Enlightened One." From that point he spent the rest of his days wandering and teaching his disciples until his death as a result of mushroom poisoning in 480 B.C. His ashes have been scattered in shrines all over Asia. Recently archaeologists believe they found fragments from the Buddha in a thumbnail size stone box southwest of Beijing.

The heart of Buddha's teaching consists of the Four Noble Truths and the Eightfold Path. All are designed to take man, in his imperfect state, to a point of perfection and enlightenment. The Four Noble Truths simply state that life consists of suffering. Second, suffering is caused by selfish desire and by the quest for private fulfillment. Third, selfish desire must be overcome, and, fourth, it can be overcome by following the Eightfold Path.

In a way somewhat similar to the Ten Commandments as a Judeo-Christian guide to morality, the Eightfold Path sets forth the moral and ethical guide of a Buddhist. The goal of the Path is to remake man through: (1.) right knowledge, (2.) right aspiration, (3.) right speech, (4.) right behavior, (5.) right livelihood, (6.) right effort, (7.) right mindfulness, and (8.) right meditation. The Buddhist way of life, in its ideal form, forbids one to kill, lie, be unchaste, or drink intoxicants.

The goal of every Buddhist is to reach that state known as nirvana (extinction) in which every fragment of desire disappears and the person is at last released from the endless cycle of birth and death. While casting aside the caste system, Buddhism maintained the concept of reincarnation or transmigration of the soul. For the devout Buddhist, there is a sense that all living things, past, present, and future, are tied together by a common thread and are constantly in a process of changing. The concept of an individual soul for each person therefore does not exist.

From its roots in India, Buddhism spread quickly into Southeast Asia, China, Korea, and Japan. By the end of the eighth century A.D., Buddhism had developed in Tibet into a mystical form called Lamaism. By the fourteenth century, Buddhism had become the official religion of Thailand. Nations such as Cambodia, Laos, and Vietnam became almost entirely Buddhist.

As the new religion spread, it also divided into several predominant sects. The Hinayana or Theravada sect is a minority grouping found primarily in Southeast Asia. Theravada Buddhism holds that only a few can reach nirvana and that such a state can be attained only through the strictest adherence to the teachings of Buddha, who is viewed as a saint, not a savior. Emphasis is placed upon a monastic life, eschewing materialism in place of austere self-discipline.

A more commonly held form of Buddhism is the Mahayana sect. Here the Buddha is viewed as a savior who is also assisted by numerous Bodhisattvas who have attained nirvana and then return to show others the way. Mahayana Buddhism takes many ritualistic forms, including lengthy ceremonies of prayers, recitations, and rituals. Mahayana Buddhism is the most commonly found sect of Buddhism in China, Korea and Japan.

However, several other forms of Buddhism have also found a place in Japan. Although originating in China, Zen Buddhism became popular among Japanese samurai beginning in the thirteenth century. Its emphasis upon courage, mind-control, and self-discipline suited the samurai life-style. Mind and body control is achieved through strict meditation, often concentrating on a *koan* or problem. Among the best known *koans* is the question: What was the appearance of your face before your ancestors were born? The discipline of Zen had an important influence on Japanese artistic expressions, including landscape gardening, the tea ceremony, and flower arranging. Even the un-cluttered, crisp lines of Japanese architecture reflect Zen culture.

A consideration of Buddhism in Japan would be incomplete without some mention of Soka Gakkai, a modern sect of Buddhism found almost exclusively in Japan. Its followers adhere to the sect of Nichiren Shoshu, a thirteenth century Buddhist teacher. Reinterpreted in 1930, the sect has grown considerably during the postwar decades. Although the original emphasis of Soka Gakkai focused on beauty and goodness, today the zealous followers have added nationalist overtones characterized by activism. Soka Gakkai appears to offer something for everyone, from concerts and ballets to education programs and mass demonstrations. Significantly, Soka Gakkai has entered the realm of politics in the form of the Komeito Party, which has gained parliamentary seats. Two motivations seem to be behind the decision by Japanese of all ages to join Soka Gakkai: anxiety about the future and the need for a sense of "belonging."

From a Christian perspective, Buddhism leaves some questions unanswered. Although Buddhism espouses selflessness and the release from desire, the goal of reaching a state of nirvana seems to be an ultimate form of selfish desire since it is a purely individual experience. Moreover, the concept of karma implies that past acts and future events are inextricably bound together, even though Buddhism suggests that nothing is permanent. If the soul is impermanent and there is no real self, how can nirvana be experienced? How can cycles of rebirth occur if there is no self to be reborn? To these questions, asked even in his own time, the Buddha was silent. Buddhism encourages its followers to find their own salvation in a highly individualistic and experiential way.

To these tenets of Buddhism, the Christian response is one of the assurance of salvation. Because of the cross that Jesus bore, all of life need not be a matter of suffering as the prophet Isaiah explained, "Surely He took up our infirmities and carried our sorrows." (Isaiah 53:4) Rather than sending each person on his own journey to salvation, Jesus issued the compelling, timeless invitation of Matthew 11:28, "Come unto me all you who are weary and burdened and I will give you rest." Essentially, Buddhism is a religion of good works in which following the Eightfold Path, meditation, and performance of ceremonies become a means to an end. Part of the essence of Christianity is that works in themselves are inadequate. "For it is by grace that you are saved, through faith, not of works, lest any man should boast." (Ephesians 2:8,9) While attempts have been made to marry Buddhist morality and meditation techniques with Christianity, the two religions are, in fact, very far apart, both in basic beliefs concerning the nature of man as well as the path of salvation.

Shintoism

Before ending a glimpse at the religions of Japan, one must briefly consider the wholly indigenous Japanese religion of Shintoism, "The Way of the Gods." Shintoism is virtually inseparable from the Japanese sense of their nation's divine creation by the gods and goddesses. Specifically, the sun goddess Amaterasu was the founder of Japan and it is from Amaterasu that the emperors were directly descended.

Through the centuries, Shintoism developed into an official state religion complete with holidays and national symbols. (The most obvious symbol is the *torii*, the gate of peace located in many cities and at the entrances of Shinto temples.) At times, the religion has been accompanied by fervent nationalism and patriotism. A more benign aspect of Shintoism, however, has been that of a catalyst for the deep reverence of the beauty of Japan. The popular pilgrimage of climbing Mount Fuji is a prominent example of the enjoyment of nature as a sacred religious experience.

Today Shintoism is not so much a strong religious movement as it is a pseudo-religious foundation for what is essentially a very secular society. Although infants are taken to Shinto shrines for blessing and some Shinto observances are maintained, in everyday Japanese life, Shintoism does not play an active role.

Chapter Seven

The Philosopher and the Prophet

Not only have Hinduism and Buddhism acted as powerful forces in Asian history, but the twin philosophies of Confucianism and Taoism (pronounced "dowism") have also played a very significant role, particularly in any area of Chinese influence. Because neither Confucianism nor Taoism deals with the hereafter or delves into theology, they are more appropriately called philosophies rather than religions.

Interestingly, Confucianism is being rehabilitated to some extent in post-Mao China as a stabilizing influence. The birthplace of Confucius is now a national shrine, a commemorative Confucian coin has been minted, and Confucian studies have been reinstituted in some universities. Vice Premier Deng Xiaoping has astutely noted that Confucianism provides a means for maintaining a sense of national order.

The fact exists that whatever China's modernizing attempts might be, the nation cannot escape the pervasive and continuing influence of Confucianism. Even Mao Tsetung, the Great Helmsman, eventually admitted that Confucian thinking could not be eradicated. Instead, he decided to use the ancient philosophy to his advantage in bringing about an acceptance of authority and uniformity of thought—both necessary for the success of his revolution. At one point, Mao went to the extreme of suggesting that if Confucius were still alive, he would be a communist.

Even in the United States the influence of Confucianism is being seen in the success of Asian American "whiz kids," the immigrant children from Japan, Korea, China and Taiwan. Sociologists have concluded that the deeply-inbred Confucianist ethic is partially responsible for the superior academic achievements of the students from East Asia.

Who was this Confucius whom historians have cited as one of the most important figures in the history of the world? Known either as Confucius or Kung Fu-tzu, he lived in Shantung Province from 551 to 478 B.C. during the chaotic Chou Dynasty. Orphaned at an early age, he later married and had two sons. Confucius was a remarkably talented man who became a tutor and city magistrate, wrote poetry, played a variety of unusual musical instruments, and was a connoisseur of fine food. He died at the age of seventy-three and was buried in the province of Lu.

To understand Confucianism, one must place the philosophy within the context of the Chinese world view and the times in which Confucius lived. The Chinese world view had been molded by the concept that the universe simply existed and that at some mystical point the earth and sky were separated. Although the ancient Chinese had a concept of a king of heaven, Shang-ti, they also believed in numerous gods and goddesses. Such beliefs are still widely held in east Asia today.

Furthermore, the Chinese traditionally viewed their nation as the Middle Kingdom (Chungkuo) in which the heavenly realm was envisioned as something of an inverted bowl from which the ancestors viewed the earth. Below heaven was China (hence the "middle kingdom") and below China was every other nation—consisting of barbarians. Such an ethnocentric view of the universe led to a sense of Chinese superiority and a xenophobia that lasted well into the twentieth century.

Such was the world view during the age of Confucius.

His era was a chaotic one in which the feudalistic system was disintegrating, peasants were heavily taxed, and the nation was in a state of anarchy, warfare, and decadence. As he viewed this state of affairs, Confucius asked the philosophical question: How can men live together in harmony?

The Confucian answer was based on the premise that man is by nature good and capable of becoming even better. While the Chinese traditionally had a concept of good and evil, there was no concept of original sin or of personal sin. Confucius, unconcerned about the afterlife, decided that if individuals were guided by moral virtue, the result would be a virtuous moral order that would not only allow men to live together in harmony but would bring about national order.

But how could personal virtue be established? Confucius answered the question with the Doctrine of the Mean, whereby men could live a balanced life in which the four passions of joy, anger, grief, and pleasure would be brought into balance. Specifically, Confucianism placed a great deal of emphasis upon the Five Cardinal Virtues of benevolence, duty, wisdom, propriety, and good manners. The virtue of benevolence was translated as human-heartedness and emphasized in Confucius' famous saying, "Do not do to others what you would not want done to yourself." The concepts of propriety and good manners eventually reached almost ludicrous heights of insistent demands. Stories have been told of the man killed in battle because he stopped to adjust the tassel on his hat, or, of the woman who died in a burning house because as a lady she could not leave unescorted. True or untrue, such stories serve to emphasize the degree to which good manners became an end in themselves in traditional China. The Confucian influence on manners can be seen in East Asia today, particularly among older people.

To preserve national harmony, Confucius placed great importance upon the stability of the family unit. The centerpiece of family relationships was the principle of filial piety in which age was venerated. Children were to be obedient, tend to parents' needs, and raise children to perpetuate the family line and bring honor to the family name. Since it was believed that the ancestors in heaven could see what was going on here on earth and thus could control earthly fortunes, the practice of ancestor worship gained importance.

These principles of propriety within the family were extended to other relationships as well. In order to live in harmony, it became necessary to exercise wisdom, courage, and compassion in five encompassing relationships: ruler to subject, father to son, husband to wife, brother to brother, and friend to friend. All human relationships fall within these five categories. If there were order in the human heart, order would exist in the family and ultimately in the nation. From the opposing perspective, if the ruler maintained personal virtue, it would permeate through the entire nation. Consequently, the emperor's responsibility was to be a virtuous "father" figure to the nation.

Certainly the Confucian virtues of filial piety can still be found in East Asia today. Family name continues to be very important. Respect for age is much in evidence whether in yielding to an elder on the subway or in allowing an octogenarian Deng Xiaoping to be Vice Premier of China.

Yet today, formerly Confucian societies are in a state of transition, particularly among educated young people. In this transitional period, Christianity can offer certain alternative answers. First, because there is no concept of original sin in areas influenced by Confucianism, (This is true in much of non-Confucianist Asia as well.) emphasis should be placed on a loving but holy God. Man stands undeserving of such love and inadequate before such holiness. Only the intervention of Christ's atoning sacrifice can allow man to stand in the presence of such a God. Man's inadequacy in and of himself is confirmed by the existence of evil in the world. Where did such evil come from? What causes man to commit evil acts or to think evil thoughts? Within the context of such questions, Biblical references such as Romans 3:23 ("All have sinned and come short of the glory of God.") and Isaiah 64:4 ("...all our righteous acts are like filthy rags.") can have practical and personal application.

As is true elsewhere in the world, the history of China and the Chinese sphere of influence is a history which displays the shortcomings and inadequacies of man. Hope is placed in man's efforts to reach perfection only to dissolve in the realization that such efforts are variable, unpredictable, and inadequate. Thus the Christian response must emphasize the absolutely unchanging and unfailing existence of a holy yet personal and loving God who has provided a way for man to have access to Him.

Taoism

Among the many changes taking place in post-Mao China is a return to the ancient, mystical philosophy of Taoism, particularly among young people who are searching for some spiritual foundation upon which to base their lives. Taoism is a uniquely Chinese philosophy which in many ways is the antithesis of communism. Since it does involve the worship of deities and includes a priesthood as well as rituals of worship, Taoism has sometimes been called a religion. Whether viewed as a philosophy or as a mystical religion, its influence has permeated Far Eastern culture.

The origins of Taoism are obscured in legend but most agree that it probably began with the teachings of the mystical Lao-tzu who predated Confucius by a half century. Taoist tradition suggests that Lao-tzu was the author of the *Tao Te Ching* in which the tenets of Taoism ("the Way") are written.

The central feature of Taoism is an esoteric concept of "tao" which is an unexplainable yet pervasive life-giving entity existing in all things. Although tao is an essence existent in everything, it cannot be put into words, a principle that is stated this way: "Those who know don't say and those who say don't know." Those who wanted to make Taoism more tangible developed what is referred to as Popular Taoism in which rituals, temples, priests, gods, and goddesses all play a role. This type of Taoism also included the use of magic, charms, and even alchemy. But for some, Taoism has remained private, individualistic, and contemplative.

Certainly Taoism has had a profound influence on Far Eastern culture. Three qualities are of particular note: non-competitiveness, humility, and simplicity. A true Taoist would not strive to be first or to better someone else. Unlike Confucianism, Taoism has little formality or rigidity. Rather, a Taoist might suggest that to do nothing is to do everything.

The Taoist influence on Chinese art can be seen in the beautiful landscape paintings that are still sought after today. The emphasis in these placid scenes is upon nature; man and his activities play a secondary role. Traditionally Taoism has encouraged man to live in harmonious balance with nature and to blend in with nature.

But one of the most significant contributions of Taoism to the Far Eastern world view is the concept of Yin and Yang. The principle behind Yin and Yang is the Taoist belief that all things are changing and therefore relative. This principle is embodied in the Yin and Yang symbol of an "s"-shaped swirl within a circle, the purpose of which is to show the perfect balance of all things. One half of the circle represents Yin, the other half represents Yang while the dots in each half suggest some Yin in Yang and vice versa. The circular shape suggests that all things are in a process of change. Thus Yin becomes Yang, Yang becomes Yin.

Moreover, the qualities of Yin and Yang are not seen as opposites but as natural counter balances to each other. For example, Yin includes such qualities as evil, passive, dark, female, winter, and death. Yang includes good, active, light, male, summer, and life. To a Taoist, good can become evil, there is male in female, winter becomes summer, and so on. All things are constantly in a process of change, thus all things are relative; nothing is absolute.

Finally, Yin and Yang is the principle behind the Chinese art of *feng shui* (literally "wind" and "water"), which combines fortune telling with geomancy. The direction to place a body in its grave, the angle to build a doorway or the shape to structure a building are all aspects of *feng shui.* The goal is to make certain that the cosmic balance of Yin and Yang is maintained at all times. Ironically, even in the planning for the impressive high-rise structures of Hong Kong and Singapore, the *feng shui* masters are consulted. Such practices reinforce the conclusion that contemporary Chinese cannot entirely escape the weight of traditionalism.

In areas of Taoist influence, what can be the Christian response? The most distinguishable difference is that of Biblical absolutes as a response to the relative concepts espoused by Taoism. The God of the Bible is an unchanging God as expressed in Malachi 3:6, "I am the Lord, I change not." He stands as an absolute standard of what is good and what is perfect. James 1:17 states the unchangeableness of God: "Every good and perfect gift is from above, coming down from the Father of the heavenly lights, who does not change like shifting shadows." To the uncertainties of a personal philosophy built upon the principle of relativism, the Christian can point to the numerous references in chapters two and three of I John which include the repeated affirmation "We know...." The Christian message in any time or any place is a message of assurance and certainty—the certainty of salvation and eternal life.

Asian Religions and New Age Philosophy

Before considering the religion of Islam, brief attention should be given to the relationship between the Asian religions and the New Age movement which is gaining influence in the West. Rudyard Kipling, the poet of the British Empire, once said, "O East is East and West is West/ And never the twain shall meet." He was wrong. East and West have met, courted and married in the form of the New Age Movement.

There is nothing new about the New Age; it is as old as the Hinduism from which it has borrowed many of its tenets. Although New Age philosophy embraces a spiritual smorgasbord of ideas, certain themes can be identified, most of which can be traced to Hinduism with some influences originating from Taoism, and Buddhism, especially Zen.

Perhaps the most central theme is monism, a concept which suggests that all is one and God is in all. Therefore New Age followers say that a transforming experience is needed for each individual in which he releases the "cosmic consciousness" already present within him. The combined releasing of energy from these collective god-like qualities in all mankind, New Age followers believe, will usher in a "New Age." Consequently, to New Agers, all religions are one and are leading in the same direction. In the words of a Japanese saying, "Many roads lead up Mount Fuji, but all reach the same top."

Not surprisingly, such ideas have made their way into science, technology, education, and even the church. Lectures on self-actualization, seminars on "management of internal resources to realize end-state visions," and articles on "visionary thinking" illustrate the subtle terminology of the New Age. More publicized have been the channeling movement, Transcendental Meditation, EST, and a series of books by Shirley MacLaine.

Not only can one see the influence of Asian religions in the New Age movement, but, from a Christian viewpoint, it becomes clear that such thinking is the antithesis of the main theme of the Gospel. The heart of the Gospel is that man, separated from God by sin, can have a living *relationship* with God through Jesus Christ. The subtle influence of the New Age serves to destroy that vital and precious man-God relationship and to make every man his own god.

Islam

If one considers Saudi Arabia as a geographic (if not cultural) part of the Asian continent, Islam is classified as an Asian religion even in its origins. Certainly Islam is Asian in its influence as evidenced by an estimated 130 million Muslims in Indonesia alone, not to mention some 300 million in South and South Central Asia. Estimates in 1987 place the world Muslim population at 900 million accompanied by a very rapid rate of growth. Huge numbers of petrodollars have been used to propagate Islam all over the world. Evidence of such investment for Allah can be seen in the shining mosques imposed upon such far-flung places as bustling Kowloon in Hong Kong, the sedate skyline of Washington D.C., or the fashionable Knightsbridge of London.

What is it that so attracts millions to Islam? The youngest of the five great religions of the world, Islam is, in many ways, the simplest in its basic theology as well as in the claims of its founder. Completely monotheistic in theology, Islam requires submission to Allah. The very name Islam (which means "submission") derives from the Arabic word *aslama* meaning "sacrifice."

Because of its Arabic origins, Islam shares a common semitic background with Judaism. Both Arabs and Jews view Abraham as their patriarch. However, whereas Jews trace their heritage through Isaac, the legitimate son of Abraham, Arabs trace their ancestral roots to Ishmael, the first-born son of Abraham. This divergence explains the 4,000 year-old argument over who ought to be the rightful heirs to the Promised Land.

By the sixth century A.D., the Arabs in and around Mecca lived in a thriving trade center—a city where believers also gathered to offer animal sacrifices to the many gods, demons and spirits of the desert. The heart of the city is the *ka'aba,* a black meteorite on which animal sacrifices were made. At Mecca, in 570 A.D., the prophet Muhammad was born. Orphaned at an early age and reared by an uncle, he later married Khadija, a wealthy woman fifteen years his senior. Although he had Christian acquaintances, Muhammad rejected Christianity as being polytheistic. To him, the concept of the Trinity implied the worship of three gods.

But Muhammad also rejected the animistic nature of Meccan religion. Instead, he frequently went out to the desert to meditate where, according to Islamic tradition, he was met repeatedly by the angel Gabriel who told Muhammad to "recite." Muslims traditionally believe that even though Muhammad was illiterate, he was given the inspiration to write the Koran (Quran). Although Muhammad's wife quickly converted to the new faith, at the end of three years, Muhammad had attracted fewer than forty converts. This fact was partly because Meccans feared the loss of revenue, particularly associated with the sacred ka'aba, if a monotheistic religion replaced their animistic beliefs.

In 622 A.D., in an event known as the Hejira and marking the year one of the Islamic calendar, Muhammad was invited to come to Medina, a city located about 200 miles north of Mecca. There Muhammad became both a political and a religious leader. Under his theocratic rule, the entire city converted to Islam. With Muhammad at its head, an army from Medina marched to Mecca, besieged the city, and took possession of the ka'aba, marching around it seven times. The entire city converted to Islam.

Although Muhammad died in 632, within a century the world's fifth great religion spread to Persia, Syria, Palestine, Iraq, Egypt, northern Africa, and into Spain. Its European advance was halted only by the historic Battle of Tours (Poitiers) in 732. By the fourteenth century Islam had become a dominant religion in India and soon made its way to China, Indonesia, and the Philippines. To Muslims, the rapid spread of Islam was "Allah's will" but a more likely explanation exists in two conditions of the time: a power vacuum existed which was filled by Islam and Muslims often forced conversions at the end of a sword.

The Koran provides the basis for Islamic belief. To a Muslim, the book is infallible and is viewed as a completion of the Torah and the Bible. Its 114 chapters, written in Arabic, form a rhythmic chant when read aloud. Three themes dominate the Koran: the concept of one god, the belief in a final judgment, and the existence of a heaven and a hell.

The single strongest tenet of this growing religion is the belief in Allah. To a Muslim, Allah is all powerful, the creator, the lord of all, holy and omniscient. Allah is, according to a frequently used analogy, closer to a Muslim than the veins in his neck. The relationship of a Muslim to Allah is one of submission to the all-knowing will of Allah. A Muslim frequently prefaces a statement of intent with the submissive phrase, "If Allah wills...." The will of Allah forms the framework for the Koran.

Although in different versions and interpretations, some Biblical stories are found in the Koran, including the story of Adam and Eve, that of Abraham (offering Ishmael), and that of the birth of Christ. Muslims perceive Jesus Christ as a prophet in line with Moses and Isaiah but suggest that Jesus' prophetic ministry was incomplete, to be fulfilled later by Muhammad. The Islamic view of Christ's death is that the crucifixion was an execution, not an atoning sacrifice. One Islamic theory holds that Christ was whisked away from the cross and a substitute, perhaps Judas, nailed to the cross in Christ's place. To a Muslim, that God could become a man and sacrifice Himself, is unthinkable.

Unlike other Asian religions, Islam has no place for reincarnation or esoteric concepts. Each person has an individual soul which must be placed in the hands of Allah. Every man is responsible for his own deeds and will stand in judgment before Allah to receive his due reward or punishment.

In order to eternally escape the punishment of hell, the devout Muslim tries to live his life according to the Five Pillars, the spiritual guideline that forms the heart of Islam. The first pillar is the creed which simply states, "There is no god but Allah, and Muhammad is his prophet." To say this and believe it makes one a Muslim.

The second pillar is that a Muslim must engage in prayer five times a day. A visitor to an Islamic city will most certainly hear the prayer call of the *muezzin* (caller) as it emanates from a *minaret* (tower) of a mosque calling the faithful to prayer. Such prayers are to be repeated upon rising, at noon, mid-afternoon, after sunset, and before retiring. Having first undergone a ceremonial washing, a Muslim then goes through the ritual prayer positions while facing toward Mecca. While many Muslims forego the practice of prayer five times a day, almost all pray on Friday, the Islamic holy day. Prayers and Koranic readings are recited in the mosque, a temple of worship, usually beautifully decorated in Arabic architecture but containing no furnishings except carpets on which to kneel for prayer. The Koran strictly forbids making any graven images of the Prophet or deifying him in any way; thus one never sees statues or pictures of Muhammad. (This is also one of the reasons Muslims object to their religion being referred to as "Muhammadanism.")

The third pillar of Islam is *zakat,* the giving of alms. Unlike the Judeo-Christian tithe, this donation is usually two and one-half per cent of one's wealth each year. The money goes to help the poor, to propagate Islam, to build and maintain mosques, and to help the needy make their pilgrimage to Mecca.

The pilgrimage to Mecca constitutes the fourth pillar of Islam and represents the spiritual summit in the life of a Muslim. Once in a lifetime, if he is able, a Muslim must make the *hajj,* the pilgrimage to the holy city of Mecca, a city completely off-limits to non-Muslims. There the faithful change into long white garments, reenact Hagar's search for water, make an atonement for sins, and visit the tomb of Muhammad. But the most important ritual of the twelve-day visit is that of walking around the ka'aba seven times. On the seventh encirclement, the Muslim must touch or kiss the sacred black stone. Thereafter in his life, he is referred to as a *hajji* and is treated with some deference.

The last of the Five Pillars requires Muslims to observe the month of Ramadan, the sacred month of fasting. Ramadan, observed throughout the Islamic world, is designed to reinforce the submissiveness and self-discipline required of a Muslim. From sunrise to sunset, Muslims fast but may eat after sunset. Consequently, in many Islamic areas, shops remain closed and transactions halted during the daylight hours but activities resume after sunset. Ramadan ends with the week of *Eed,* a week of festivities and gift-giving.

To the Five Pillars of Islam, some have suggested there is an additional "sixth pillar," *jihad.* Jihad, which means "striving for god," is often called "holy war" because the Koran promises heaven to anyone who dies while defending the faith. Consequently, fanatical acts sometimes take place in the Islamic world. Young boys throw themselves before murderous artillery fire in the Iran-Iraq war, and terrorists allow themselves to be killed while hijacking an airplane or attacking a military base in Beirut—all in the name of jihad. The commitment to jihad has been spreading in conjunction with the rising influence of militant fundamentalist Islam.

In addition to these Islamic principles are other practices, some of which can be traced in origin to the Koran or to the *Shariah* (law based on tradition). Female infanticide is forbidden as is the consumption of alcohol or the practice of gambling. A man may marry up to four wives if he treats them equally. The practice of *purdah* (wearing of the veil) is still practiced by many Islamic women as an act of submission and modesty.

However, as is true with other religions of Asia, Islam has another side. Beneath the observance of The Five Pillars, at the most basic level in villages and homes, the religion often becomes "Folk Islam." Folk Islam includes traditional animistic beliefs, superstitions, a fear of spirits, and practices of magic. Such folk practices are not always readily observable from the more orthodox Islamic exterior, but present the missionary with an added spiritual hindrance that requires understanding.

Today, Islam may well be the world's most formidable challenge to Christianity. Not only is it growing rapidly, but is becoming increasingly militant along with employing aggressive proselytizing techniques. Yet, Islam is by no means monolithic. Muslims are divided into various sects (Shiite, Sunni, and Sufi) as well as by geography, language, and culture. A Muslim woman in Kuala Lumpur may be well educated, dressing in fashionable western style clothing, while her Islamic sister in Pakistan still wears the veil.

Nor is the Islamic world a closed door or an impossible mission field. In fact, new opportunities exist for sharing the Gospel as ideological struggles occur in the Islamic world. Restlessness, especially among young people, has produced areas of openness and of receptiveness to the teachings of Christ. Moreover, the Islamic mission field is now found everywhere since Muslim students, refugees, immigrants, and business men are scattered all over the world. Los Angeles, London, and Paris represent Islamic mission fields as surely as do Hyderabad, India and Jakarta, Indonesia.

From a Christian perspective, the Koran can actually be used as a bridge on which to share the Gospel because it has already introduced Muslims to Jesus. It is the person of Jesus Christ as Savior of the world to whom Muslims have not yet been introduced. The voluntary nature of Jesus' sacrificial death must be clarified as in John 10:14, "...I lay down my life for the sheep," and again in verse eighteen: "No one takes it from me, but I lay it down of my own accord. I have authority to lay it down and authority to take it up again." The sacrificial death of Jesus must be presented to the Muslim as the greatest single act of love in all of history.

Furthermore, the personal and intimate character of God as a Father is a missing element in the relationship between most Muslims and Allah. Because it is Jesus, the Son, who came to reveal the Father's heart to mankind, a rejection of Jesus as the incarnate Son means a loss of that intimate revelation of God as a Father, a revelation that brings spiritual fulfillment to every human being, whatever his status.

Finally, the most effective proof to Muslims is tangible evidence of lives transformed through Jesus Christ. No greater evidence of the power of the cross is there than the love of Jesus as manifested through another human being. This is most obvious in the slow but fruitful process of friendship evangelism, an evangelism that is often the best strategy in Islamic areas. Interestingly, South Korean Christians have achieved considerable success in sharing the Gospel in Islamic areas of the Middle East. Such sharing dramatizes that the Kingdom Culture, a culture which bridges cultural differences, is being established worldwide.

Chapter Eight

A Cultural Mosaic

How dull the world would be if everyone looked the same, dressed the same, ate the same kind of food and lived in the same kind of houses. Cultural differences have characterized the world since the time the descendants of Shem, Ham and Japheth, Noah's sons, dispersed out into the world from the Near East. The multiplicity of cultures in Asia bears witness to the creative nature of an infinitely imaginative God. These very cultural differences, that lend interest and variety to God's world, however, present the missionary with one of his most formidable challenges.

While suggested definitions of the word "culture" abound, perhaps the term can simply be summarized as referring to the acquired ways of behavior in a given society. The culture of any given group includes everything from religion and language to the dress, mode of living, mores, and values of a particular people. Culture maintains the unusual element of being transmitted from one generation to another, over a long period time, often in unspoken and subtle ways.

For the Christian, it is of utmost importance to remember that the Gospel, while often applied within cultural patterns, in itself belongs to no specific culture because of its distinction as a divine revelation. Yet, the Gospel belongs to all cultures. The Holy Spirit, now uniting Christians all over the world, does not carry a passport, or require a visa. A Kingdom Culture is being established which encompasses people of every society and nation yet is characterized by certain Biblical common denominators—the most basic of which exists in the commitment to Jesus Christ, a commitment expressed in many different ways and in many different languages.

One of the most decisive Biblical statements about the nature of the Kingdom Culture came after Peter's experience at the home of the Gentile, Cornelius. In Acts 10:34-35, Peter proclaimed, "I now realize how true it is that God does not show favoritism, but accepts men from every nation who fear him and do what is right."

Later, in Jerusalem, Peter reiterated this principle of God's acceptance of people from all nations. Standing before the Jerusalem meeting, Peter stated, "God, who knows the heart, showed that He accepted them by giving the Holy Spirit to them just as He did to us. He made no distinction between us and them, for He purified their hearts by faith." (Acts 15: 8-9)

With this understanding in mind, how can a person approach a culture different from his own, particularly when the goal is to share the Gospel? One key lies in learning as much about that culture as possible. The Old Testament offers two relevant examples of young men transplanted to other cultures who learned a great deal about their new environments. After being sold by his brothers into the land of Egypt, Joseph not only lived in the house of an aristocratic Egyptian, but we may also assume that he dressed in the Egyptian style, learned the language of the nation, and gained an understanding of the culture. Proof of this is the elevated position of trust he attained as chief advisor to the pharoah. However, one significant difference prevailed between Joseph and the people among whom he lived— Joseph never abandoned the faith of his Hebrew forefathers; he remained true to the Lord.

In similar fashion, Daniel, after being transplanted as a young man from Judah to Babylon, soon was selected to receive special training and education. The first chapter of the Book of Daniel tells us that he was to be trained in the language and literature of the Babylonians. But like his forefather Joseph, Daniel never allowed himself to be defiled by the evil aspects of the culture to which he had been transplanted. Because both Joseph and Daniel remained true to their faith, God caused them to be looked upon favorably by influential persons of another culture.

Learning about another culture is not the only key to effectively sharing the Gospel. Certain other responses also help to bridge cultural gaps almost universally. One of the foremost of these cultural responses is respect. I Peter 3:15 tells us that we should "...be prepared to give an answer to everyone who asks you to give the reason for the hope that you have. But do this with gentleness and respect." Respect takes into consideration the world view held by someone from another culture. Respect responds with sensitivity in recognizing the pride of ownership another person possesses toward his own culture. Respect acknowledges that God has the same amount of love invested in every human being on earth. Respect esteems another as better than oneself.

Close companion of respect is interest. To express a genuine interest in another person, whatever his culture, accords him value. Such interest, in effect, says, "You are important enough that I want to know something about you." Jesus set such an example when He demonstrated the same interest to each one of a broad cross section of persons including tax collectors, children, the woman taken in adultery, the Samaritan woman at the well, and wealthy Nicodemous who visited Jesus at night.

Because common values exist almost universally, whatever the culture, pertinent subjects of genuine mutual interest always exist. A parent or grandparent in China or Thailand is as eager to talk about his offspring as a parent or grandparent in Canada or Denmark. Similarly, every farmer in the world discusses the weather, soil conditions, weeds, and insects. Not only can interest be shown within the context of shared values, but an expressed interest about the very areas that make someone culturally different can become a key response and an avenue for sharing.

A similar important response when placed in another culture is flexibility. Outsiders cannot insist upon having their own rights when in another culture. To expect that circumstances, particularly in a developing nation of Asia, should be altered for the comfort of someone from a developed nation is contrary to the very Gospel intended to be shared. The attitude with which the bearer of the Gospel responds to cultural differences may well speak far more loudly than a message shared verbally.

Finally, perhaps the most encompassing response to another culture is an attitude of love. The great love passage found in chapter thirteen of I Corinthians leaves no room for condescension or disdain. The mark of the Christian is not only to love those of another culture, but also to love his own co-workers. More than one missionary endeavor has deteriorated into ineffectiveness because co-workers gave ground to petty differences when placed within a new cultural setting. Love should be the umbrella under which all sharing of the Gospel takes place. The issue need not be made more complicated than one overriding fact. Love covers.

Asian Cultural Characteristics

The evolution of the global village has considerably blurred East-West differences. The use of the term "East-West" as a strict dichotomy no longer applies as accurately as it once did. Cross-cultural exchange between Asia and the rest of the world is increasing at a rapid rate.

Moreover, the complex cultural mosaic that comprises Asia does not easily lend itself to generalizations. For example, the value system of Indians in the state of Kerala obviously would be very different from that of Singaporean Chinese. Furthermore, the rate of cultural change and the degree of contact with the rest of the world varies from place to place in Asia.

Nevertheless, certain widespread, notable cultural characteristics of Asia still remain to a significant enough degree to warrant consideration, particularly by someone from the West who might be going to Asia on a missionary endeavor. Seven general cultural differences between Asia and the Western world are considered here.

One major cultural difference lies in the non-confrontational tradition of Asia when compared with the confrontational tradition of the West. Generally speaking, Asians place a greater premium on "maintaining one's place" in society. Wives are more submissive to husbands, students are less likely to confront teachers, young people show more respect toward the elderly. In traditional Asian settings, particularly in rural areas, a far greater acceptance of one's lot in life exists. The Hindu concept of karma, which influences over 800 million people of Asia, leads to the complacent acceptance of class placement by birth. In the huge area dominated by Chinese culture, the traditional Confucian principles of a structured society, veneration of age, acceptance of authority, and uniformity of thought are still in evidence.

Ironically, particularly in densely populated Japan does "maintaining one's place" appear to be unusually important. Indeed, the exquisite politeness and respect with which the Japanese treat others may well be partially attributable to centuries of living in small rooms separated by paper-thin walls. In personal relationships, the Japanese seem to find it easier to deal with each other on an unequal basis rather than on one as equals. Titles, company names, age, and one's sex can all play roles in establishing the basis for a transaction. Many Western businessmen attempting to transact negotiations in Japan have almost given up in frustration at the slow, ritualistic, and vague methods used by their Japanese counterparts. The concept of *haragei* plays an important role in transactions and relationships. *Haragei* can best be translated as an unspoken understanding or silent agreement, a subtle concept difficult for Westerners to understand.

On a larger scale, evidence of the non-confrontational tradition in Asia includes the fact that fewer law suits occur, divorce is much less common, and labor strikes are infrequent. A strongly developed two-party political system is non-existent in most Asian nations, while in others such a system constitutes a relatively new concept. Even in Japan and South Korea, where demonstrations sometimes occur, they are led by uncertain young people who are in a transitional phase between traditionalism and modernization.

Closely related to this tradition of non-confrontation is a second major cultural difference separating Asia and the West—that is the characteristic attitude of reserve in Asian manner as compared with the openness Westerners display. In Western society, particularly in recent decades, the practice of "expressing one's self" has gained importance. Psychologists encourage clients to express their repressed feelings. Public opinion polls show the man-on-the-street criticizing national leadership. Strangers in crowded airports exchange angry words.

However, in many Asian nations, particularly those of East Asia and Southeast Asia, a quiet reserve reigns in situations that a Westerner would find intolerable. Packed subways, long lines in railway stations and ferry landings, jostling crowds on the streets are all greeted with calm acceptance. A wife rebuked by her husband or a daughter-in-law berated by her mother-in-law responds with silence. This acquired trait of self-control often derives from a carefully cultivated and disciplined inner strength, particularly in East Asia.

Consequently, an understanding of the Asian traditions of non-confrontation and reserve are essential to sharing the Gospel in a sensitive fashion. The missionary must exercise care not to present the Gospel in a manner that could be perceived as confrontational. Moreover, upon sharing the Gospel, the missionary may be met with signs of courtesy and respect that can be misunderstood to indicate acceptance. The young Taiwanese nodding in agreement may be saying, in effect, "I see," rather than "I agree." He does not want to be disrespectful by saying "no," nor does he want to be confrontational by engaging in debate.

A third major cultural difference between Asia and the Western world is that of identification as part of a group in contrast to the Western emphasis upon individuality. From Switzerland, to the United States, to Australia, Westerners traditionally place great value on independence. The image of the self-made man perpetuates itself in folk tales, biographies, and movies. History books acclaim rugged individualism and frontier spirit as essentials that built nations.

In Asia, however, from villages in South India to automobile factories in Japan, the custom is that the individual identifies himself as part of a group. Security, pride, and loyalty derive from a sense of belonging and of contributing to a whole. Consequently, conformity within the group and maintaining dignity before the members of the group take on great significance.

This group identification begins within the family, then moves outward to friends, clan, tribe, village, caste, and finally to religion. In urban areas the tribe and village identification may be supplanted by association with fellow workers and the company. Whereas in India one might say, "He is a Brahmin," in Japan one might say, "He is a Mitsubishi man." The concept remains the same in that the point of identification rests in some form of group.

One of the roots of such group identification in areas influenced by China can be traced to the Confucian era. The Confucianist concept of harmony and balance within a society was based upon cooperation and upon the belief that an ordered society equals a peaceful society. The Confucianist ideal consisted of a hierarchical society in which each person maintained his proper place within the group. Today, some two thousand years later, the Confucianist influence persists.

In Japan, the word which best describes the concept of group identification is the word *uchi*, which means "within." The sense of belonging, of being within, is particularly strong in Japan, whether that means being part of a school, belonging to one of Japan's many clubs, or a member of the company for which one works. The high suicide rate in Japan is largely attributed to the shame a person feels when he believes he has embarrassed or disappointed his family, friends, or larger group.

Consequently, when an Asian who has a strong group identification becomes a Christian, his decision affects not just himself, but it affects his whole group. He may risk ostracism from his family, friends, tribe, or caste. For example, a young Christian convert in Calcutta finds that she has been cut off from her caste and told that her family will no longer arrange a marriage for her. In China, a Christian factory worker is denied promotion as a subtle form of discrimination. Such actual stories are multiplied throughout Asia because many who come to the Lord must do so at considerable personal cost.

A fourth major way in which Asian culture differs from the West lies in the tradition of authoritarianism which prevails in Asia as compared with the democratic tradition of the West. Historically, the democratic tradition of the West traces its path from the Greeks and Romans, through the Renaissance and Reformation, and into the Enlightenment. Transmitted by educated men, the concept of individual freedoms was perceived as a natural birthright of every human being. The right of the citizen to freely elect a government hierarchy that would then protect the rights of the people became a pillar of democracy.

In Asia, such a tradition never developed. Rather, the historical legacy consists of emperors, monarchies, and tribal or clan chieftains. Even during the period of European colonialism, Asians gained little experience in democratic traditions. Consequently, when independence came to the former colonies during the postwar era, little preparation had been made for democracy Authoritarianism simply continued in new forms.

In Singapore, Lee Kuan Yew has been the only Prime Minister since the nation's independence. Elsewhere in Southeast Asia, the picture has been one of dictatorships and strongman rule, producing such names as Ho Chi Minh and Pol Pot. Indonesia has been dominated by one president, General Suharto, since 1968. In the Philippines, the world is watching a significant experiment as a people's revolution that rejected the excesses of Ferdinand Marcos struggles to implement a democracy under Corazon Aquino.

Meanwhile, in North Korea, Kim Il Sung remains the only leader the nation has known since its inception. In Taiwan, Chiang Ching-kuo simply took over at the death of his father, Chiang Kai-shek, and ruled until his own death in early 1988, whereupon he was replaced by Lee Teng-hui, a committed Christian and who may bring about some political reform.

In China, where the imperial system was replaced by the "Great Helmsman," Mao Tse-tung, the pattern of authoritarianism continues under Deng Xiaoping, albeit a somewhat more enlightened authoritarianism. Even in India, which prides itself on being the world's largest democracy, the political tradition since 1947 has been that of a dynasty. The prime ministership remains in one family, from Jawaharlal Nehru, to his daughter Indira Gandhi, to her son Rajiv Gandhi.

In light of such a tradition, however, the recent politics of two Asian nations are noteworthy. Following World War II, the occupation forces established democratic procedures in Japan which have succeeded for the most part. Although a succession of short-term prime ministers has occurred, the democratic process remains secure.

However, in South Korea the conflict between authoritarianism and democracy is now seen openly. The political legitimacy of the existing government is being challenged in ways that appear to conflict with traditional Asian cultural standards. Strikes, riots, and violence have broken with the characteristic reserve and respect so much a part of the Confucian legacy. Student-led protests indicate that Korean young people are undergoing a transitional stage in which they are breaking with traditional principles in their desire to grasp a democratic ideal.

The fifth major cultural difference between Asia and the Western world is the concept of time and everything related to it. Westerners are time conscious to an extreme. Expensive watches adorn wrists while an imaginative array of clocks can be found on mantels, auto dashboards, classroom walls, and bank buildings. Promptness is viewed as a virtue even to the extent of being a criterion for evaluating job performance.

Not only are Westerners very clock conscious, but they also place a great deal of importance on historic dates. Students find history boring because they are required to memorize dates. Every English child knows what happened in 1066 just as every student in the United States knows the significance of 1776. Those Americans who were alive on November 22, 1963 have forever fixed in their memories their exact location when they heard of the assassination of John F. Kennedy. Calendars in the Western world are filled with days commemorating events of past dates.

In Asia, however, the general occurrence is far more important than the specific date. After all, nations such as China and India measure their histories in millenia, dynasties, and epochs. While American historians may speak of the eight year administration of a president, the Chinese make reference to the T'ang Dynasty (a period of almost three hundred years) or to a whole imperial cycle. On a continent that is still predominantly rural, time relates to monsoon cycles and to the ebb and flow of the seasons. On a daily basis, a meeting or appointment is more likely to be viewed as a general happening rather than as a specific goal to be reached by 1:30 p.m. Many an exasperated

Westerner has fretted impatiently after calling a meeting for 7:00 p.m. only to discover that at 7:15 no one has arrived. If he let patience win, he no doubt discovered that his meeting was in full attendance by 8:00 p.m. However, one exception to this general Asian time orientation should be noted—Japan. Not surprisingly, punctuality is important in the nation which produces a sizable portion of the world's watches and clocks.

A sixth major cultural difference between the Western world and Asia lies in the way in which prestige is bestowed. Because Western culture is strongly performance oriented, public recognition goes to individual achievement. Athletes compete for trophies, actors strive for academy awards, academics earn college degrees. Social mobility allows a person to work his way "upward," the rewards for success being wealth, fame, and power. Winning automatically awards prestige to the winner.

In Asia, prestige derives, for the most part, from entirely different sources. Status comes from such sources as caste, family name, and tribe—all positions into which one is born. To be born a Brahmin in India bestows immediate prestige, even on a baby. In Southeast Asia, to be the son of a village chief or headman translates into power. Furthermore, traditional relationships bring prestige to certain positions. For example, teachers are accorded prestige and respect from students. Spiritual leaders such as *gurus,* priests, and shamans also enjoy prestige and status. Finally, age is venerated in Asia in a way very unlike age is treated in the West. Simply stated, the older a person is in most parts of Asia, the more respect he or she receives.

Finally, the seventh major cultural difference between Asia and the West is the way in which moral and ethical standards are viewed. In the Western world, standards of law and justice or of right and wrong are seen as absolutes. The concept of absolute standards can be traced back to the Judeo-Christian foundations which influenced Western law. A strongly developed definition of what constitutes good and evil carried over into accepted models of behavior and social responsibility. In the West, the concept of sin not only is widely recognized, but, within certain parameters, carries a generally accepted definition.

Unfortunately, in recent decades, the Western world has also seen a gradual erosion of absolute standards of right and wrong or of what finds definition as acceptable or unacceptable. For example, the decisions pronounced in several Western nations concerning abortion and euthenasia reflect a move toward relative ethical thinking, in this case, pertaining to the most basic issue of what consitutes human life.

Such relative thinking is more in keeping with the way in which standards are viewed in Asia. Whereas Western reasoning suggests that rational responses exist for everything, Asian thinking suggests that there are no absolute answers. Rather, Asians view the world as being dualistic. The universe consists of complimentary forces which balance each other to produce a harmonious dichotomy. Moreover, all things are constantly changing, whether seen through the Yin and Yang framework or as part of the cycle of karma. What is good can become evil and what is evil can become good.

Furthermore, while Asians may have a concept of evil, the notion of sin, particularly of personal sin, is far less often recognized. Consequently, shame becomes a more common response to wrongdoing than does guilt. Certainly an understanding of these relative assumptions is indispensible in effectively sharing the Gospel throughout much of Asia.

Not surprisingly, as the global village extends itself, these seven cultural differences between Asia and the West become less pronounced. Many of the cultural characteristics of the West, such as performance-based prestige and time orientation, seem to accompany modernization, particularly in those areas where modernization has become identified with westernization.

Asian Artistic Expressions

In Asia, artistic expression is nearly inseparable from religion. Even in secular societies such as China and Japan, if the roots of artistic representation are traced, they quite likely are Buddhist or Taoist. Furthermore, art, in all its forms, is a basic means of human expression throughout Asia and constitutes an integral part of life from city to village. Whether through temple architecture, sculpture, painting, drama, dance, or movies, the visitor to Asia is surrounded by reminders of how great a role the arts play in Asia. The missionary who ignores such an essential component of Asian culture overlooks a potential avenue for sharing the Gospel and is insensitive to a very important aspect of Asian life.

Perhaps one of the most widespread forms of art in Asia is sculpture. Most Asian sculpture can be categorized as either Brahmin or Buddhist. Brahmin sculpture, associated with Hinduism, may seem confusing and sensuous to the Western eye. Hindu sculpture attempts to show unity in diversity, a reflection of the relative thinking discussed earlier. For example, Hindu sculpture may possess both male and female characteristics. Gods may be depicted with several faces in an attempt to convey more than one divine attribute. Or a Hindu sculpture of a deity may possess several pairs of arms, thus conveying the concept of omnipotence. The overall goal of Brahminic sculpture is to bring the divine world of the myriad of Hindu gods and goddesses down to the level of man's understanding. Perhaps the most famous example is that of Shiva, the destroyer, dancing on top of the world. Such sculptures become the objects of ritual worship even to the extent of being bathed, clothed, and fed by the worshippers. This is particularly true of revered sculptures located within certain celebrated temples.

Buddhist sculpture invariably depicts either the Buddha or one of the numerous bodhisattvas who lead others to nirvana. Most often, Buddhist sculpture shows the Buddha or bodhisattva in the serene state of nirvana reflected in a sublime facial expression, although several unusual sculptures of the Buddha show him in an emaciated state of prolonged fasting.

As to be expected, Buddhist art began in India and underwent subtle variations as it made its way eastward. As Buddhism inched into Southeast Asia, China, Korea, and Japan, regional, racial, and ethnic changes appeared. During the centuries that have followed, the Buddha has been depicted as a reclining Buddha, a laughing Buddha, and, most often, a Buddha seated in the lotus position. At Kamakura in Japan, the largest Buddhist sculpture in the world shows the venerated religious leader seated in the lotus position, thumbs touching in the meditative connection of the finite with the infinite. One characteristic dominates these sculptures: the Buddha poses in a sublime state of nirvana.

This characterization contrasts sharply with Christian artists' portrayals, particularly during the Medieval and Renaissance periods, of the suffering Christ, who bore the sins of the world on His own body. The prophet Isaiah describes the suffering Christ in Isaiah 52:14, "...His appearance was so disfigured beyond that of any man and His form marred beyond human likeness."

From a Christian perspective, Buddhist and Brahminic sculptures in Asia stand as reminders of the truth stated in Habakkuk 2:18-20. "Of what value is an idol, since man has carved it? Or an image that teaches lies? For he who makes it trusts in his own creation; he makes idols that cannot speak. Woe to him who says to wood, 'Come to life!' Or to lifeless stone, 'Wake up!' Can it give guidance? It is covered with gold and silver; there is no breath in it. But the Lord is in His holy temple; let all the earth keep silence before Him."

Closely related to the art of sculpture is the temple art of Asia. Again, India serves as the source of inspiration for most temple art. Although regional variations exist, most temples were built according to a rigid scheme designed to show the balance and order of the cosmos. Hindu temples in India are often dedicated to a god or goddess and are almost always maintained by priests from the Brahmin caste. The elaborate pantheon of gods and goddesses carved along walls and rooflines presents an overwhelming and confusing sight to the Western observer.

As temple art spread from India eastward, architectural styles changed. At the famous site of Angkor Wat in Cambodia, the largest of the magnificent temples consists of walls within walls within more walls adorned with fifty-four elaborate towers. Further eastward, Chinese and Japanese architects adopted the graceful multi-storied pagoda style of curved rooftops for most temples and shrines. Often a rectangular court precedes entrance to a main hall topped with as many as four or five stories.

While pagoda temples in China represent a major art form, they are by no means China's only major artistic contribution. Chinese craftsmen became masters at using the beautiful jade found in riverbeds. Sometimes called the "stone of heaven," jade was accorded the five Confucian virtues of charity, rectitude, wisdom, courage, and justice. Centuries-old jade carvings, often unbelievably detailed and intricate, are among China's most highly prized art collections.

Similarly, the Chinese maintained no peers in the production of fine porcelains. Known throughout the world as "china," these translucent masterpieces set the standard for the rest of the world. As early as 2,000 B.C., Chinese potters were firing clay at extremely high temperatures, then finishing their handicrafts with glaze. Although T'ang porcelains are the most refined, Ming porcelains are the most renowned because of their delicate blue and white colorations.

Closely related to the Chinese production of porcelains has been the continuing art form known as cloissonne. Although the term is French and the art form made its way to China via the Near East in the fourteenth century, Chinese experts adopted the method to such a high degree that cloisonne is regarded to be a Chinese art. During the process, brightly colored enamel designs are separated by fine metal bands then covered with a glaze that produces a glassy texture.

But the Chinese art form that has maintained the timeless quality of bringing pleasure to generations of on-lookers is that of landscape painting. Here both Taoist and Buddhist influence can be discerned. The landscapes are contemplative, meditative, and peaceful. Scenes capture an unrecurring moment in nature such as a bird resting on a bough. Human activity, if included, plays a very insignificant and almost hidden role. Most of the skilled Chinese landscape painters worked from images lodged in their memories and did not attempt to recreate specific locations. The materials were almost always the same: brushes, various colors of ink, and silk paper. Most landscape paintings were intended to be "read," often with a poetic inscription at the beginning or ending. Although painting became stylized under communist rule, many beautiful landscape paintings remain from previous centuries, the best being from the Sung Dynasty of the eleventh century.

Although sculpture, architecture, and painting form a major portion of Asian artistic expression, drama and dance are of equal significance in many areas. They are similarly religious in nature. Most commonly, drama and dance combine to tell a story in which good inevitably triumphs over evil. In India alone, over forty different dance/drama forms exist, often with regional distinctions. Said to be originated by the gods, most act out epic stories from the Hindu *Ramayana* and *Mahabharata*. Based upon an elaborate system of body movements—particularly those of head, hands, and feet—classical Indian dance remains a great source of cultural pride.

In Thailand, classical dance/drama also represents a national cultural treasure. Here, females often play male roles, and dialogue is sometimes spoken, supplemented by a female chorus at the side. As in India, hand, eye, and head gestures convey subtle meanings which must be closely watched by the audience. In another form of Thai classical dance, males wearing masks reinact battles while a narrator relates a famous epic.

The Japanese have, in characteristic fashion, maintained traditional drama forms within a culture of high technology. Two ancient drama forms, *noh* and *kabuki,* still draw sell-out audiences. *Noh* drama, with its slow, perfectly controlled movements and exaggerated voice tones of actors, reflects the disciplined qualities of Zen. Actors, wearing striking masks depicting certain human emotions, reenact the suffering of warriors and court ladies until redeemed by the love of the Buddha. *Noh* dramas, performed on a bare stage with a minimum of props, often last three or four hours.

By contrast, *kabuki* dramas are noisy, flamboyant, and raucous. Elaborate costuming and grand sets (often utilizing the latest technology) make *kabuki* performances a feast for the eyes. *Kabuki* dramas, which usually combine history, dance, and even an occasional domestic sequence, may last as long as five hours.

One other very unusual form of drama should be noted: the masterful puppetry of Malaysia. Malaysia, a Southeast Asian meeting ground of various cultures, is the home of shadow puppetry on a grand scale. The puppets, often larger than life, are controlled, not by strings from the top as are marionettes, but by sticks from the bottom. The puppets perform behind screens of a lightweight fabric so that the darkened silhouettes of the puppets appear before the enthralled audience. As many as two hundred or three hundred puppeteers are involved in productions that may last two or three successive evenings.

Finally, a consideration of Asian artistic forms would be incomplete without some mention of the movies of India. Movies and television are popular throughout Asia, but India is the world's largest producer of movies. With production centers in Bombay and Madras, movies are cranked out bearing a repetitious formula. Invariably, the

moviegoer can count on a love story in which good triumphs over evil. Along the way, he can expect to see
slapstick comedy, a breathtaking chase, a fight between the
hero and the villain, and a tender musical scene between
the hero and the heroine. Such Indian movies are shown
throughout Asia from crude village theaters to video
screens on noisy buses. The exception to this stylized form
of Indian movie is the documentary, a form that has
received international recognition. These innovative Indian films dramatize tough social issues such as the unjust
dowry system and prostitution. Several such documentaries
have exerted pressure for social legislation in India.

From a Christian perspective, an understanding of the
role the arts play in Asian culture can lead to the development of significant strategies for evangelism. If it is
generally true that art forms can be used for the advance-
ment of the kingdom of God, then it is particularly true in
Asia. For example, the fondness for movies provides an obvious mission strategy as verified by the eager response to
the movie "Jesus" being shown in villages throughout
India. The popularity of drama can easily become a mission
strategy when the Gospel is illustrated in the universal language of the pantomime. Certainly the increasingly
widespread access to television throughout Asia represents
a great missions opportunity for creative programming. In
China alone, the government estimates that 900 million
Chinese have access to television. This fact, coupled with
the technology of satellite communication, makes the
prospect for completing the Great Commission in Asia a
very realistic prospect in the near future.

Chapter Nine

Waging Victory

When Moses sent the spies into Canaan, as explained in Numbers 13 and 14, his purpose was not merely for them to survey the land and its productive capacity. The spies were also told to estimate how strong a foe the Canaanites might be. All twelve spies returned with glowing reports of the land of milk and honey. But the majority report stirred fear among the Israelites by the proclamation that the Canaanites were too powerful to be overtaken. Only the minority report given by Joshua and Caleb assured the Israelites that they could indeed pass into the land. What caused these two men to view the same obstacles from a different perspective? The answer lies in the overrriding fact that these two understood the character of God and His victorious power. Joshua and Caleb first looked at God, then at the goodness of the land, and finally at the difficulties in securing the land—in that order. Because of their faith they stated, "...but the Lord is with us." (Numbers 14:9)

In a similar sense, the previous chapters of this book have been a survey of the characteristics of Asia—its place within the Third World context, its geography and history, its complex pattern of religions, and its rich, fascinating culture. But another aspect of Asia exists which is not so easily captured in words—that of Asia's spiritual culture. For the Christian in Asia or for the Christian going to Asia, an awareness and understanding of Asia's spiritual climate may well be of greater importance than any other information. However, an awareness of the factors discussed in previous chapters provides a basis for understanding Asia's spiritual culture. Interestingly, the word "culture" in its Latin derivation included a linkage with the concept of "worship."

The Great Commission is most certainly being carried out, but within the context of a spiritual war for which the theater is global. Asia is no exception. To claim Asia for Christ requires engaging in spiritual warfare. Spiritual warfare for Christians resembles conventional warfare in the sense that in both types there are no rules and no one is exempt from attack. Evangelizing Asia is not for the faint of heart or for those who seek an easy task. Rather, reaching Asians with the Gospel presents a challenge to be accepted only by those bold Christians willing to take the offensive.

Certainly, the Apostle Paul makes the nature of spiritual warfare quite clear in Ephesians 6:12 when he states, "For our struggle is not against flesh and blood, but against the rulers, against the authorities, against the powers of this dark world and against the spiritual forces of evil in the heavenly realms." Just as the Israelites were forced to defeat a host of tribal enemies in order to claim the Promised Land, so Christians must contend with spiritual powers and principalities in order to carry out the Great Commission.

Spiritual Powers and Principalities

Before the characteristics of Asia's spiritual atmosphere can be understood, the nature of spiritual powers and principalities should be examined. What are these entities, where did they come from, and how do they operate?

The fourteenth chapter of Isaiah describes the great rebellious upheaval that took place in heaven at some point during the eons of time past. Lucifer, a beautiful angel, aspired to exalt himself above God. Isaiah 14:12-14 recounts this cataclysmic event: "How you have fallen from heaven, O morning star, son of the dawn! You have been cast down to the earth, you who once laid low the nations! You said in your heart, 'I will ascend to heaven; I will raise my throne above the stars of God,... I will make myself like the Most High.'"

Jesus Himself, who was with the Father from the beginning, watched Satan's expulsion from heaven. He told His disciples, "I saw Satan fall like lightning from heaven." (Luke 10:18) Not only was Satan expelled from his heavenly abode, but he was accompanied by a huge force of accomplices consisting of one-third of the angels. In the twelfth chapter of Revelation, Satan is referred to as a dragon cast out of heaven, whose tail swept a third of the stars (angels) with him. In Matthew 25:41, Jesus' statement makes clear the intended destination of Satan and his angels, "Then He will say to those on His left, 'Depart from Me, you who are cursed into the eternal fire prepared for the devil and his angels.'"

Consequently, Lucifer and his fallen angels have become the ruling prince of darkness and the principalities and powers mentioned by Paul in Ephesians 6:12, previously quoted. I John 5:19 states that the evil one controls the earthly, temporal systems. The Apostle writes, "We know that we are children of God and that the whole world is under the control of the evil one."

However, in this titanic struggle within the universe between the Kingdom of Light and the Kingdom of Darkness, the most glorious news is that Jesus Christ triumphed over Satan and his evil angels at the cross. Colossians 2:15, tells the victorious news of what Christ did: "And having disarmed the powers and authorities, he made a public spectacle of them, triumphing over them by the cross." Since the sacrifice at Calvary, Satan has been a defeated foe.

If Satan is defeated, why must Christians still contend with such an adversary? The answer can best be given in the analogy of warfare. Although a foe can be defeated in battle, it takes some time before he is actually disarmed and military action can stop. For example, historians have generally agreed that Napoleon's defeat came in 1813 during his disastrous winter campaign in Russia, but not until 1815 were the Napoleonic battles ended at Waterloo. In spite of the fact that Satan is defeated, he is determined to wreak as much havoc as possible in his defeat.

Not only are Christians fighting a foe whose defeat has already been sealed, but Christians have also been equipped with weapons of warfare that are spiritually tailor-made for spiritual warfare. First, Christians are given the armor of God, which really is a way of life, but is described in the military analogy as being the belt of truth, the breastplate of righteousness, the shoes of readiness, the shield of faith, the helmet of salvation, and the sword of the spirit, accompanied by praying in the Spirit. (Eph.6:13-18) In addition, Christians have been assured that their weapons are spiritual, not temporal. II Corinthians 10:14 declares, "The weapons we fight with are not the weapons of the world. On the contrary, they have divine power to demolish strongholds."

These strongholds constitute the spiritual domain of the principalities and powers of darkness. In Asia, as well as elsewhere in the world, these spiritual powers have established themselves in environments that are conducive to their *modus operandi.* Where temporal institutions and systems exist apart from Godly principles, a conducive, welcome environment is created for the prince of darkness to associate himself in order to link his spiritual power with earthly, temporal power. One goal exists: to maintain power at all costs.

Consequently, sharing the Gospel and establishing the Kingdom of Light in the world must involve the bringing down of false spiritual strongholds. This task is accomplished, not by concentrating upon the power of the enemy, but by the realization of the greatness of God's power and by calling upon Him to manifest His mighty power. Such knowledge becomes the foundation for a whole victorious Christian lifestyle over which Satan can have little influence.

Through appropriating the power of the Word of God and through united prayer, Christians can rob Satan of his possessions and destroy his dominions. For such united prayer, Asian Christians themselves present an interesting model. From churches in Singapore to cell groups in Seoul, Christians often pray in groups, in unison, aloud, and for the same prayer topic. Such aggressive, fervent prayer changes nations.

Spiritual Strongholds in Asia

In Asia, as elsewhere in the world, the discerning Christian can identify the particular dominating spiritual powers by means of the revelation of the Holy Spirit and by identifying certain geographic and cultural characteristics of a given place. Such knowledge brings about an important awareness for the Christian's own spiritual protection and contributes greatly to the planning of mission strategy.

For example, the Christian can recognize that a large city which stands as a center of banking, commerce, manufacturing, and trade, provides the temporal environment for the spirit of mammon with all of its associated activities of greed, dishonesty, and competition. Such characteristics are then manifested at a very personal level in the lives of the people of that city. Inhabitants or visitors may find themselves caught up in frenzied buying and selling, competitiveness, or dishonesty. Christians can then pray specifically that the power of God will be manifested in such a way as to break the stronghold of mammon over that city.

Elsewhere in Asia, cities with universities, colleges, or a tradition of literary achievement provide the conducive temporal environment for the spiritual stronghold of intellectualism with its accompanying characteristics of pride, arrogance, and sophistry.

Moreover, geographic, historical, religious, and cultural heritage combine to play an important role in determining the spiritual dominions over defined areas. Certainly this is as true of Asia as it is elsewhere in the world. Such dominions are powerfully and firmly established over a period of many years, decades, and even centuries, therefore influencing one generation after another.

For example, from a geographic perspective, the fact that a nation or a particular part of a nation is an island can provide the spiritual climate for a feeling of isolation which in turn may produce a sense of low esteem on the part of the nation or the persons living in that nation. Conversely, the sense of isolation bred from generations of island living may lead to a spirit of superiority, exclusiveness, or pride. A similar situation could exist in areas cut off from the rest of the world by mountain ranges, deserts, or bodies of water.

Furthermore, the long history of a nation prepares the foundation for certain spiritual characteristics. Both a spirit of rejection and a strong spirit of independence can be the spiritual bequest of a nation that was once a colony of another, more powerful, nation. Certainly the historical legacy of Asia includes various forms of colonization and domination. The spiritual heritage of a nation once conquered in war or occupied by another power may include feelings of great sadness, heaviness, and a desire for self-protection. Fear becomes a spiritual stronghold clutching a nation torn by war such as that in Southeast Asia.

Furthermore, a nation which has a lengthy heritage of economic deprivation and struggle for existence then becomes the temporal environment for a spirit of poverty which grips people in a cycle of hopelessness, apathy, resignation, and despair. Regrettably, this condition characterizes the spiritual climate of much of Asia and represents a major stronghold to be brought down by aggressively praying Christians. Ironically, a state of poverty can also be the abiding place of a spirit of materialism whereby the desire for accumulation of material goods, even at the most rudimentary level, becomes an intensely sought after objective.

Another historical factor which can play a role in the spiritual culture of a nation is the influx of refugees. Recent events in Afghanistan and in nations of Southeast Asia forced a massive movement of people from their homelands to other nations. Refugees carry with them a sense of rejection which can then influence the spiritual environment of the nation to which they have fled. Likewise, the spiritual milieu of a nation of immigrants becomes a heterogeneous combination of contributing factors ranging from the religious to the social and cultural. Disunity and disharmony can become major spiritual obstacles in nations where many languages are spoken.

Finally, of course, the dominant religious forms of a nation contribute greatly to the nature of prevailing spiritual principalities. Polytheism, animism, spiritism, the practice of witchcraft, and the occult provide welcome environments for the activities of the rulers of darkness. Fear, deceit, and darkness can then become the dominating spirits. A religious spirit constitutues a major, very powerful spiritual stronghold over those nations and regions that have a legacy of strict, almost unanimous religious participation such as in Hindu, Buddhist, and Muslim nations.

Because of the forceful influence of predominant religions in most Asian nations, Christians should bear in mind one of the restrictions placed upon the Israelites when they were about to go into the Promised Land. While engaged in spiritual warfare and while in the midst of a spiritual culture alien to the Kingdom Culture, Christians are exhorted not to allow themselves to be defiled by evil influences. When the Israelites were about to take the land of Canaan, Moses cautioned them about maintaining their own spiritual purity, particularly in the area of possessions.

In Deuteronomy 7:25-26, a very important restriction was placed upon the activities of the Israelites. "The images of their gods you are to burn in the fire. Do not covet the silver and gold on them, and do not take it for yourselves, or you will be ensnared by it, for it is detestable to the Lord your God. Do not bring a detestable thing into your house or you, like it, will be set apart for destruction. Utterly abhor and detest it, for it is set apart for destruction."

How is this scripture applicable to Christians today? The same principle of spiritual defilement applies today as it did to the Israelites. Often through a combination of naivete, curiosity, and even the purchase of souvenirs or the purpose of education, Christians acquire items which have religious meaning and then place those items in their homes or give them as gifts. For example, statues of Buddha or Shiva; cloisonne, porcelain, or silk items decorated with the Chinese dragon; bells, joss sticks, musical instruments, or other items used in religious rituals; masks, clothing, or artifacts of tribal religious practices all represent contemporary items that are, in the words of the Deuteronomy passage, "...detestable to the Lord your God."

Likewise, a word of caution is in order concerning Christians who wander into temples, mosques, shrines, and other places of religious significance. At such sites, the powers of darkness gather in greater intensity and concentration than elsewhere. Even the most mature Christian, with the best of intentions, by himself, is no equal to the magnitude of demonic activity that often exists in such places, particularly in polytheistic Hindu areas. Spiritual warfare, if it is to be carried out in such places, should be done only by concerted group effort by mature, knowledgeable Christians in a united, aggressive strategy.

Results of Spiritual Warfare

The powerful spiritual victories obtained through the efforts of praying, steadfast Christians changes tribes, cities, regions, institutions, and nations. Historically, whole wars ultimately are won by the accumulation of individual skirmishes and battles. So it is with spiritual warfare. The evidence of such separate spiritual victories, won over a period of many years, can be seen in many parts of Asia.

In Burma, at least six tribes are now predominantly Christian. The Kachin tribe alone has over 100,000 believers, some of whom were baptized, along with 6,000 others, in a single baptismal service in 1971. In the northern state of Nagaland in India, an estimated 80 percent of the population of almost one million is Christian following a major revival that swept through the area between 1976 and 1978. This revival was followed by a collective, solemn pledge on the part of Naga Christians to engage in a concerted program of evangelization.

South Korea had no churches a hundred years ago. Today the capital of Seoul alone has over 6,000 churches. Estimates in South Korea today suggest that over 30 per cent of the populace is evangelical Christian. Almost half of the Korean army is Christian while the Parliament can claim that fully one-third of its members are Christian. The Full Gospel Central Church of Pastor Yonggi Cho is approaching a membership of over 500,000. Pastor Cho and other Christian leaders of Korea have given much of the credit for the miraculous change taking place in their nation to the effectual, fervent prayers of believers, a great many of them devout, dedicated women who steadfastly intercede for their nation.

But perhaps the most astonishing proof of the victorious power of Christ manifested in Asia as a result of determined, committed, praying Christians is the church in China. Through the 1950's and 1960's, the church was persecuted and forced underground, an event leading the outside world to fear that the Chinese church had all but disappeared. When it resurfaced in the early 1980's, the world was atonished to learn what the Holy Spirit had done. Not only was the church of China alive, but it was exceedingly well, dynamic, and growing. Today, the estimate of 50 million Christians in China may well be a conservative one.

Unquestionably Christians, both individually and collectively, are engaged in spiritual warfare. Ground is either being gained or lost. No demilitarized zone exists in spiritual warfare. In Asia, the powers and principalities of darkness are being pushed back, territory taken, societies and ancient cultures changed. The day of complete victory in Christ is near and will be hastened as Christians take the offensive, praying the Lord of the harvest to send forth laborers.

The victory that will come in spiritual warfare is spoken of in Isaiah 41. There, in verse 12, the promise is given: "Though you search for your enemies, you will not find them. Those who wage war against you will be as nothing at all. For I am the Lord, your God, who takes hold of your right hand and says to you, 'Do not fear; I will help you.' " In verses 15 and 16, the promise of power is phrased in the analogy, "See, I will make you into a threshing sledge, new and sharp, with many teeth. You will thresh the mountains and crush them, and reduce the hills to chaff. You will winnow them, the wind will pick them up, and a gale will blow them away. But you will rejoice in the Lord and glory in the Holy One of Israel." To those who may be battle weary, Paul offers these reassuring words in Romans 16:20, "The God of peace will soon crush Satan under your feet."

What then is the result of bringing down the principalities and powers of darkness in Asia? The tearing down process is executed so that a building-up process can take place similar to the process described by the prophet Jeremiah over 2,500 years ago. He wrote: "See today I appoint you over nations and kingdoms to uproot and tear down, to destroy and overthrow, to build and to plant." (Jer. 1:10) What is that building-up process taking place in Asia? It can only be the glorification of the one true God, the Father of all mankind.

Chapter Ten

Success Demands Its Price

When Paul wrote to Timothy, he exhorted the young man to pray for kings and rulers. In I Timothy 2:1-2 we read: "I urge, then, first of all, that requests, prayer, intercession and thanksgiving be made for everyone—for kings and all those in authority, that we may live peaceful and quiet lives in all godliness and holiness." Clearly Paul placed a high priority on prayer on behalf of rulers and others in authority.

For us as world Christians, this passage suggests the need to pray not only for our own governmental leaders, but also for those of other nations. The Bible clearly establishes that governing authority is ordained by God. Romans 13:1 instructs that, "Everyone must submit himself to the governing authorities, for there is no authority except that which God has established."

Because God maintains sovereignty over all mankind, He can as easily remove someone from power as allow him or her to maintain power. Whether the leader be Deng Xiaoping of China, Mikhail Gorbachev of the Soviet Union, or Margaret Thatcher of England, God is true sovereign and arranges the affairs of nations in accordance with a divinely-ordained destiny.

This Biblical passage assures us that the events of Asia do have meaning insofar as they contribute to God's ultimate plan for Asia. Nothing happens by accident. Moral, spiritual, economic, and political forces come together in accordance with God's sovereign will. Therefore, Christians should pray with understanding, with specificity, and in accordance with God's will as instructed by the Holy Spirit. Praying specifically and with understanding comes as a result of being informed and aware of issues and events.

Today, as Asia stands on the brink of its last decade in the twentieth century, three major trends emerge to form the framework within which most Asian nations will make future decisions. First, a newly educated and growing middle class questions the political legitimacy of many Asian governments. Not only is Asian leadership aging, but it also maintains political power through questionable processes. Military coups, one-party electoral systems, or family dynasties characterize the basis for authority of a significant number of Asian leaders.

The second major trend in Asia is that of growing regionalism, based upon racial or ethnic differences, which threatens the unity of many Asian nations. The re-emergence of old religious rivalries and ethnic disputes presents a marked destabilizing factor. In still other regions, fundamentalist and communist insurgencies jeopardize the effectiveness of legitimate governments.

Third, all Asian nations must respond to economic challenges. Problems vary from the seemingly hopeless economic situation of Bangladesh to the hugely successful economy of Japan, which now demands a system of controls. In between these extremes, other Asian nations face economic issues largely centered around the appropriate use of basic natural and human resources. As a whole, however, the rate of economic growth in Asia exceeds that in most other areas of the world. On balance, there is reason to be cautiously optimistic about Asia's future. However, a look at the contemporary issues of selected nations or regions will provide a clearer picture of the Asian scene.

China

China presents an enigmatic yet endlessly fascinating portrait to the world. Although China, shut off by itself for years, flung open its doors to the rest of the world in 1979, much of the enigma remains. China appears involved in a frenetic attempt to leap from antiquity to modernity. Yet the phrase "two steps forward, one step backward" aptly describes the style of Chinese evolutionary change. China does indeed have a great deal of catching up to do. In 1949, Mao Tse-tung declared the establishment of the People's Republic of China. Yet that same year, footbinding was still being practiced in some remote areas of China—and at the same time the Western world was entering the atomic age.

The present scene in China becomes more meaningful when considered in relation to the Great Proletarian Cultural Revolution which occurred between 1966 and 1976. During that time, the aging Mao, determined to maintain his grip upon China and ensure an ongoing communist revolution, unleashed the energy of millions of young people known as the Red Guards. The ten year period of national frenzy was directed toward eradicating any vestiges of pre-revolutionary China. Intellectuals, artists, and Christians were particular targets for persecution.

Not surprisingly, the economy suffered severe setbacks as did educational and cultural institutions. Moreover, China isolated itself from the outside world, thus falling further behind in terms of modernization. But perhaps the greatest wound of all was to the national spirit. Virtually every Chinese family experienced some form of negative fallout from the Cultural Revolution.

Mao's death in 1976 stunned the nation; the man who had occupied the position of a god turned out to be a mere mortal. In their search for some semblance of stability, the Chinese now turned to a man once disgraced during the Cultural Revolution—Vice Premier Deng Xiaoping. Although Deng traced his philosophical roots to membership in the Chinese Communist Party as early as the 1920's, he not only exhibited an amazing capacity for survival, but he maintained reformist ideas.

Thus by 1978, China had embarked on a revolutionary new course enunciated by Deng in the form of the "Four Modernizations." The proposed goal was that, by the year 2000, China should catch up with the West in four strategic areas: defense, industry, science, and agriculture. In an attempt to close an era, the Cultural Revolution was blamed on the notorious "Gang of Four." Even Mao himself was dethroned and characterized as a well-intentioned leader but capable of making mistakes.

Unquestionably, China's accomplishments since 1980 are impressive. China's per capita rural income has tripled while per capita income in cities grew almost as much. National income during 1986 alone increased 7 per cent. Much of this has been due to limited economic freedoms, most notably the production responsibility system whereby individuals may contract with the government to produce a certain quota. Anything produced beyond the contracted quotas may be sold and the money kept by the producers.

The system has succeeded remarkably well in rural areas where the breakup of communes and the introduction of incentives now make Chinese farmers among the most efficient in the world in terms of output per acre. This new but limited economic freedom can also be seen in cities where innumerable sidewalk capitalist enterprises offer everything from cabbages to nylon racing jackets to sunglasses.

Moreover, the Chinese cultural scene now bears incongruous touches of the global village. Maxim's French restaurant and Colonel Sander's Kentucky Fried Chicken now advertize their cuisine in Beijing, where once the daily greeting was "Have you eaten today?" The monotonous unisex Mao suits are gradually being replaced by blue jeans, skirts, and multi-colored blouses. A refrigerator, washing machine, and TV set represent the three most desirable purchases to people both in cities and rural areas.

Beijing even boasts of a newly completed subway system.

However, beneath the impressive economic growth and veneer of cultural change lies a host of thorny problems. A rise both in inflation and in the trade deficit represents a major economic dilemma. Foreign investors no longer find China such an alluring market in which to place their investment capital.

But beyond these economic issues, certain political, moral, and cultural issues present even greater challenges. Chinese leaders must resolve what appear to be irreconcilable differences. Can economic freedom be allowed without accompanying it with political freedom? Can small-scale capitalist enterprises exist within a socialist system? Must China westernize in order to modernize?

Behind these broad dilemmas rests another, more specific question: What will happen to China after Deng Xiaoping? The diminutive octogenarian claims that he is gradually withdrawing from leadership. Accordingly, at the Thirteenth Party Congress, held in October of 1987, a new generation of leaders assumed power positions, thus replacing many old-line Maoists. Power now rests in the hands of a five-man Standing Committee of the Politburo led by Zhao Ziyang. Although the new guard are younger and more moderate, to call them "liberals" would be a mistake. Rather, they are "reformers."

Outside observers must not be deceived into thinking that China is changing colors. Evidence of China's firm commitment to communism came when, at the Thirteenth Party Congress in 1987, Deng reiterated the four inviolable principles of China's future course: socialism; the dictatorship of the proletariat; communist party leadership; and Marxist, Leninist, Maoist thought. Restrictions in 1987 against student freedoms, artistic experimentalism, and intellectual criticism indicate that an undercurrent of repression still exists.

Young people of China now seem particularly vulnerable to disillusionment and apathy. While they desire to see China grow strong and become an important part of the international community, many young people are disillusioned with the Communist Party which, they believe, has failed the people through unfulfilled promises. Consequently, the youth of China, particularly in cities, are embracing a self-serving philosophy of materialism. A sizable portion of young adults, born during the Cultural Revolution, seem to lack a sense of purpose and direction. Those somewhat older, who were among the Red Guards of the 1960's and 1970's, are also among the disenchanted. Corruption, bribery, and other types of crime are now a reality in a nation that prided itself on the elimination of crime after 1949.

But from a Christian perspective, the church of China ranks as the single most significant aspect of contemporary China. Despite persecutions of Chinese Christians since 1949 (most severely during the Cultural Revolution), the Chinese church may well be one of the most dynamic churches in the world today.

Actually, two churches exist in China: the official church and the underground church. The official church of China started in the 1950's under the government name, Three Self-Patriotic Movement (TSPM). The government insisted that the church must be "self-supporting, self-propagating, and self-governing." Under the leadership of Bishop Ding, the TSPM has sponsored the reopening of churches in addition to eleven official seminaries. Certainly devout, sincere Christians make up an important part of the TSPM. Three Self church services each Sunday usually have standing room only, so great is the spiritual appetite of a people long suppressed.

However, the TSPM presents a deceptive exterior. Some TSPM pastors, are forbidden to mention four topics from the pulpit: the return of Christ, suffering for Christ, casting out of demons, or healing of the sick. Other official restrictions include the forbidding of religious meetings in any places other than those designated by the government; forbidding baptism to anyone without first undergoing questioning about motives and political attitudes; forbidding possession of religious literature, including Bibles, not printed in China. In 1987, the TSPM leadership suggested that China's Christian population numbered approximately 3,000,000; hence the proposed printing of 500,000 Bibles in China per year is sufficient.

In reality, the Christian population of China is vastly larger because the underground church—the other church in China—numbers from 30 to 50 million believers and possibly as many as 100 million. The underground church of China, meeting in homes, abandoned buildings, storage facilities, and anywhere else available, bears the distinctive marks of a church that has undergone the purifying refinement of suffering and even of martyrdom. Those who were Christian during the Cultural Revolution discuss imprisonment, beatings, and persecutions as being a normal experience in their suffering for Christ. Characterized as a praying, praising, reverent, and witnessing church, the Chinese church today strongly resembles the early church described in the book of Acts. Not surprisingly, the Chinese church is also a fervently evangelistic church where miracles regularly occur.

However, even when considering what appears to be a new religious freedom in China, the outside observer should not be misled. An undercurrent of repression remains in which some Christians are persecuted in a variety of subtle ways aside from the restrictions mentioned earlier. Loss of jobs and discrimination in housing are just several of the ways Christians face obstacles because of their faith.

Furthermore, two major problems exist in the home church of China. First, the supply of Bibles and other Christian literature is grossly inadequate throughout the nation. Chinese Christians, especially in rural areas, must share one Bible for as many as 1,000 to 2,000 people. Obtaining a Bible from the officially China-published supply of Bibles requires bureaucratic registration and a long waiting period.

Second, the rapid growth of the Chinese church

presents the desperate need for pastors, teachers, and lay leaders capable of discipling new believers. At present, many pastors of the underground church try to serve more than one church, often going from one to another by bicycle and usually visiting each church only once per month or even less. Both of these requests—for Bibles and for workers—represent specific, pressing items for prayer and intercession among world Christians.

Certainly, we are in an era of unprecedented opportunity in China. Relations with the Western world remain open; the nation stands ready and open to outside influence; a large population of young people in China are seeking something in which to anchor their faith. Buddhism, Confucianism, Taoism, Marxism, Maoism, and Christianity represent philosophical forces tugging at the minds of millions of Chinese.

Christians should pray specifically that the hearts of the men now in the vanguard of China's new leadership will be softened and made sensitive to the spiritual needs of China's people. Prayer should be directed toward the formulation of policies that will provide a stable, peaceful China where the church can grow and mature.

The recent history of China reveals a record of sudden turnabouts in policy reflecting the communist Chinese view of change as an inevitable part of a dialectical process in which nothing remains static. China-watchers in the West and in Hong Kong still raise the possibility of China's once again retreating from its path of openness. Certainly the situation in China suggests the reality of Christ's words, "As long as it is day, we must do the work of him who sent me. Night is coming, when no man can work." (John 9:4)

Japan

Like the mythical phoenix rising from the ashes of its own destruction, Japan has risen from the rubble of World War II to become the second greatest economic power in the world. The object of both admiration and resentment, this small group of islands set in the Pacific Rim can be likened to no other nation on earth.

Today, Japan blends an extraordinary combination of high technology and modernization with distinctive characteristics of custom and traditionalism. The mixture often presents a picture of apparent contradictions. Perhaps nowhere in contemporary Japan is this incongruity more apparent than at Tokyo's Disneyland, which has taken on the attributes of a national shrine. There a kimono-clad grandmother may have her picture taken in the embrace of Mickey-san (Mickey Mouse). Even Emperor Hirohito, the living symbol of Japan's glorious imperial past of shoguns, samurai warriors, and pagoda temples, wears a Mickey Mouse wristwatch.

Yet, the Japanese passion for things Western is not entirely a new phenomenon. Japan has long exerted an amazing capacity for change. In 1858, following 250 years of isolation from the rest of the world, Japan quickly abandoned its feudal traditions and rushed wholeheartedly into borrowing from the West in order to modernize.

What is new however, is that Japan now walks on new and untried territory. Japan is a nation searching to know itself, for Japan now finds itself in the position of a world leader, an uncomfortable role which it seems reluctant to accept. Simply stated, the greatest challenge facing Japan today is the challenge of success. Japan is discovering what history has shown elsewhere: success demands its price.

Japan's success is almost entirely economic. As the only nation other than the United States with a gross national product of over one trillion dollars per year, Japan's trade surplus in 1986 alone amounted to $83 billion. Japan's economic influence further extends itself through the multi-billions of dollars of Japanese capital invested abroad. Yet, Japan must import nearly all of its oil, natural gas, and coal in addition to a great amount of its foodstuffs. Moreover, the nation is a collection of islands whose total territory would fit inside the U.S. state of Montana. Yet, Japan must cram its 120 million people into only 18 per cent of that land because mountains prevent settlement of the remaining area.

With all of these handicaps, how has Japan managed such an economic miracle? First, behind Japan's driving force stands the principle of consensus whereby individuals are bound together in a sense of common purpose. Second, from its earliest contacts with other nations, Japan borrowed and emulated. In a sense, Japan has allowed the rest of the world to serve as a global research laboratory from which Japan has sought out and adopted the best from abroad. Third, despite their deeply ingrained principle of consensus, the Japanese are fierce market competitors, within their own country as well as abroad. Fourth, the pressure of competition boosts the level of quality control. Even Western consumers now are inclined to purchase Japanese-made goods on the basis of proven superior quality. Finally, Japan's economic success results from a strong desire to provide security for the future. Investors and workers alike forego quick profits today in exchange for long-range prosperity. From the highest level of the government all the way down to individual levels, saving money is held as a staunch principle of economic well-being.

However, Japan must now pay a high price for such success. Japan's trading partners are forcing Japan to open its own doors to more foreign-made goods. Competition increases from other Asian nations such as Singapore, Taiwan, and South Korea where goods can be manufactured more cheaply than in Japan. Foreign competition in such Japanese industries as shipbuilding and steel production have actually forced lay-offs where once a job was assured for a lifetime.

At a deeper level, the Japanese must undergo a basic change in the introverted way in which they view themselves as being different from the rest of the world. A new term has crept into the Japanese vocabulary, *kokusai-ka,* which means "internationalization." Japan's position in the world now demands that it genuinely enter the world community by allowing foreign investment within its own borders and by accepting international responsibilities.

From a Christian perspective, however, issues and trends exist within contemporary Japan which suggest a society in transition. Consumerism is becoming a national neurosis. The traditional "we" generation in which group identity is uppermost is being challenged by a growing "me" generation of young people bent on immediate gratification. Japan's older generation looks with alarm as the rate of juvenile delinquency increases each year. A society which emphasizes mass conformity, particularly in its restrictive, pressurized educational system, appears to be producing a rebellious discontent among young people.

At the opposite end of the age spectrum, the elderly of Japan find themselves in a position unprecedented in Japan's long history. Because of longer life expectancy and lower birth rate, the size of Japan's elderly population expands each year. By traditional Confucian values, such a large elderly populace would be considered of great value. However, in contemporary Japan, where energies are almost solely devoted to work, the elderly feel alienated and isolated. Because of the acute housing shortage and small living space per family, care for the elderly presents a serious challenge for the future.

Finally, women in Japanese society constitute a third group in transition. Equality for women within the strict confines of Japanese culture continues to be a difficult goal to attain even though the constitution provides for legal equality. Marriage remains the most important goal of young Japanese women in a system where over half of all marriages are arranged.

However, after marriage, the life of a Japanese woman centers around child care and household tasks. In an effort to limit the size of their families, two out of every three Japanese women of child-bearing age have undergone at least one abortion. Husbands, occupied by their jobs, spend little quality time at home. Consequently, after children are grown, Japanese housewives, with much time on their hands, often feel their lives lack meaning and fulfillment.

Spiritually, Japan remains an amalgam of traditional religions. Newborn infants are taken to Shinto shrines for a blessing from a Shinto priest. However, at the time of marriage, many young couples prefer the symbolism and customs of a Christian ceremony. Then, at the end of life, most Japanese request Buddhist funerals. Although the nation claims to be both Shintoist and Buddhist, in reality, less than 30 per cent of the nation's population profess any personal religious beliefs. Less than one per cent profess to be Christian and many of those stray away from the faith due to societal pressures. New religions, such as the militant Sokka Gokkai, are attracting increasing numbers as people try to fill the spiritual vacuum in their lives.

Christian missions in Japan face formidable challenges. The complex culture presents level upon level of intricate subtleties, many of which complicate communication. Understanding is made even more difficult by the exacting written and spoken language which requires a lifetime to master. The Christian church of Japan reflects the formality of Japan's secular society. Church attendance is low, a circumstance complicated by the fact that adult males have so little free time.

Yet, opportunities for sharing the Gospel do exist. Disillusioned young people, alienated elderly, bored housewives, and an overstressed work force represent specific groups for which mission strategy is needed. Not only should world Christians pray for such strategy, but they should also pray for unity and a new vitality in the existing Japanese church. Prayer should also be directed towards the provision of increased finances for mission enterprises in Japan where living costs are among the highest in the world.

South Korea

During the last half of 1987, the world watched in astonishment as Korean university students lobbed stones and Molotov cocktails at police fully clad in medieval-looking riot gear. The protests symbolized one of South Korea's major problems—the need for political modernization. South Korea is a microcosm of the problem facing other newly industrialized nations of Asia. Dynamic economic growth accompanied by a literate, educated middle class has outgrown the traditional Confucian model of benevolent but authoritarian-style government. Political modernization has failed to keep pace with economic modernization.

South Korea's economic growth ranks as an Asian marvel. Following the Korean War of the early 1950's, the wartime devastation placed South Korea among Asia's other Third World nations. In 1960, the per capita income was a mere $82 per year. By 1987, the annual per capita income stood at $2,500, making South Koreans well-off by Asian standards. South Korea also boasts a high literacy rate of 98 per cent. Moreover, economic growth rate and a rising standard of living in South Korea show little sign of slowing.

How did such an economic miracle take place in South Korea? When the government of President Park Chung Hee came to power in 1961 following a military coup, the government initiated a massive program of foreign borrowing and private investment. The nation capitalized on the availability of a highly motivated work force willing to work at low wages. Soon South Korea exported inexpensive goods, particularly textiles, which presented strong competition for Japanese or Western-made goods. So great is South Korea's exporting success that other nations have considered protectionist policies in response.

Despite its amazing economic success, South Korea must cope with other problems. The presidential election of December, 1987 threatened to be another rubber-stamp move on the part of the government and thus took place in an atmosphere of violence and confrontation. Protesting university students garnered support from religious groups, businessmen, and housewives in their anti-government demonstrations.

However, the larger than anticipated margin of victory of Roh Tae Woo, the government candidate, indicated the voters' desire for stability. Nevertheless, Roh's is a minority presidency. Three opposition candidates actually split a combined total of over 50 per cent of the vote, a figure representing a large element of the populace that did not vote for the present government.

The world must hope that South Korea will enter an era of political reconciliation. The ever-present specter of North Korea in the background represents a threatening factor. An unstable political situation in Seoul might tempt Kim Il Sung, the aging and authoritarian communist leader of North Korea, to launch a military maneuver into South Korea, an action which could draw the superpowers into an Asian war. Furthermore, South Koreans very much desire to present a picture of their country to the world as a stable, forward-looking, world class nation. Nothing so symbolizes South Korean pride as the scheduling of the 1988 Summer Olympics in Seoul.

From a Christian perspective, South Korea must best be viewed as a nation in transition with all of the problems associated with such an era. Politically, the nation is undergoing an uncertain transition from authoritarianism to democracy. Economically, South Korea is moving from underdevelopment to being predominantly urban and industrially developed.

As a result, the youth of Korea have caught a glimpse of what the future might hold but they want to grasp that future now. In exchange for a rise in living standards, the adult work force must work long hours at low wages. During such a transitional period as South Korea is now experiencing, the elderly, their feet set in Confucian traditionalism, watch with confusion, wonderment, and uncertainty at the changes taking place in their nation—a nation which has only recently known the great suffering of war.

But South Korea also stands as a nation in which Christianity is a truly significant factor. In a country with strong Buddhist, Confucianist, and Taoist ties, some 30 per cent of the populace now claims to be Christian. Furthermore, their Christianity reaches far beyond mere declaration of faith. South Korean Christians are prayer warriors, both in the amount of time spent in prayer and in their fervency of spirit. Their famous prayer mountains, in which facilities are provided for persons desiring to spend many days in prayer, are indicative of the priority placed on prayer. Korean women participate, not only in prayer, but in other spiritual responsibilities to a far greater extent than their Asian counterparts.

A key factor to the strength of the Korean church lies in the concept of cell groups, a practice which strengthens close fellowship and takes advantage of the Korean gift for hospitality. The Korean church places great importance upon personal experience and upon the manifestations of God's power through the Holy Spirit.

Finally, the South Korean church is a missionary church in which high priority is placed upon sending missionaries both throughout South Korea and to some 47 other nations. With generous financial support from tithing Christians, the goal of South Korean mission organizations is to send 10,000 missionaries to other nations by the year 2000.

However, Christians need to pray for the continued spiritual fervency of the South Korean church. Success carries temptation with it as does increased materialism. Already, liberal theology is making inroads in some areas of the Korean church. These problems aside, however, the South Korean church represents a compelling spiritual force and a vital part of Christianity today.

Chapter Eleven

One Treaty and Two New Faces

Few places in Asia give such a vivid impression of optimism and confidence as does Hong Kong. Skyscrapers under construction stand encased in their antiquated bamboo scaffolding. A scan of the horizon reveals a varied collection of high-rise apartment buildings solidly clustered on rocky hillsides. Rolls Royces, Bentleys, and other luxury automobiles vie with an endless line of red taxicabs for control of congested streets. Every conceivable type of merchandise from the largest to the smallest can be bought or sold in Hong Kong's fiercely competitive arena of free enterprise and endless pursuit of profit.

However, Hong Kong's confident exterior conceals a somber realization lodged in the backs of the minds of all Hong Kong residents. On July 1, 1997, the British Crown Colony of Hong Kong must be handed over to the People's Republic of China. From corporate board rooms to back room factories, that single fact overshadows all plans and thoughts about the future of Hong Kong.

The diplomatic background which set the stage for the 1997 transition actually dates all the way back to 1842. Following a British victory in the first phase of the so-called Opium War (1840-1842), the Chinese submitted to the Treaty of Nanking which, among other provisions, ceded the island of Hong Kong to Great Britain "in perpetuity." Subsequently, in the Convention of Peking (1860), China ceded the Kowloon Peninsula—also "in perpetuity." Then, in 1898, Great Britain leased the 365 square mile area known as the New Territories, plus 235 adjacent islands, for a period of 99 years. While Hong Kong Island and Kowloon form the heart of the Hong Kong colony, the leased territories provide necessary land for agriculture, industry, a large containerport, and several approaches to Kai Tak airport. Simply stated, Hong Kong cannot maintain viability without the New Territories.

Thus, in 1982, when Great Britain opened discussions with China concerning the future of the New Territories, all of Hong Kong was, by necessity, placed on the negotiating agenda. The negotiations dragged on for several years, ending officially in December of 1984 with the signing of a Joint Declaration by Prime Minister Margaret Thatcher of Great Britain and China's Premier Zhao Ziyang. During the entire negotiating process, frustrated Hong Kong residents watched helplessly due to the fact that they were given no direct voice in the discussion process and therefore little voice in the determination of their future.

Of course, the heart of the Joint Declaration lies in the agreement to turn all of Hong Kong over to mainland Chinese ownership in 1997. The greatest concession won by the British negotiators was an agreement by the Chinese that Hong Kong's economic, social, and legal system will not be changed for a period of fifty years after 1997. Among other important provisions of the agreement is the promise to allow freedom of press, speech, assembly, travel, occupation, and religious belief. Private property and ownership are to be protected by law.

Missing from the Joint Declaration was an explanation of the Basic Law describing the nature of the post-1997 Hong Kong government. Furthermore, the Joint Declaration did not address the thorny issue of the future citizenship for over 2,000,000 of Hong Kong's 5.5 million residents who do not hold British passports. Nor did the agreement make any mention about the conscripting of Hong Kong youths for the armed forces.

The response from Hong Kong has been varied. Most of Hong Kong's populace have adopted a wait-and-see attitude, while many entrepreneurs have embraced a "get all you can while you can" philosophy. Some residents who can afford to do so plan to leave Hong Kong before 1997. A government survey revealed that fully 70 per cent of persons in the 15 to 24 age group would like to leave if they could. Most, however, cannot leave and must hope for the best.

Certainly an economically healthy Hong Kong is in China's best interests. Although Hong Kong depends on mainland China for water and a great portion of its food supply, China derives financial benefit from investments and trade with Hong Kong. If Hong Kong's economy slumps before 1997, it is highly unlikely that it would regain viability after the takeover. Moreover, China would be much less likely to interfere with a prosperous Hong Kong.

Nevertheless, a cloud of uncertainty remains over Hong Kong. The Chinese Communist Party has quietly expanded its membership in Hong Kong while Chinese leaders have let it be known that party politics will be unwelcome after 1997. One Chinese fear seems to be that Taiwan may try to influence Hong Kong politics against China as a means of creating problems for the mainland. Taiwan and Hong Kong presently maintain a close trading relationship, a situation which raises serious questions for the economic future after the mainland (with whom Taiwan has no relations) takes control of Hong Kong. Some observers suggest that China wishes to make the transition in Hong Kong an example of what would be done in Taiwan if unification occurred as the People's Republic so desires.

Other unanswered questions remain. What might happen to the agreement after the passing of Deng Xiaoping? Will his successors honor a document signed in 1984? Does the terminology pertaining to basic freedoms mean the same to the Chinese as it means to the British? Can the Chinese allow economic, political, and personal freedoms in Hong Kong and not allow them on the mainland?

Not only does the transition affect the two major nations, but it also affects hundreds of international corporations, institutions, and organizations which have agreements with Hong Kong. Over 400 international agreements entered into by the British government in Hong Kong must be reexamined. The perspective of other Asian nations also bears consideration. Such countries as Indonesia, Malaysia, and Singapore look upon the Joint Declaration with considerable suspicion. Not only have these and other Asian nations viewed Hong Kong as a non-communist nation, but they are angry with China for its supportive role in insurgencies elsewhere in Asia. Consequently, these Asian countries may decide to break relations with Hong Kong and restrict citizens from travel there after 1997.

From a Christian viewpoint, the 1997 transition raises important questions, the most obvious of which is the issue of religious freedom. Although the government of the PRC officially espouses freedom of religion, the Christian church in China still remains the object of restrictions. Would such restrictions (see previous chapter) also be applied to Hong Kong Christians? The Joint Declaration declares specifically that religious organizations in Hong Kong may continue their association with religious organizations elsewhere and may continue to operate schools, hospitals, and welfare institutions. But they are not to interfere with or be subordinate to religious institutions on the Chinese mainland.

Some Hong Kong church officials look upon 1997 as a positive challenge for several reasons. First, faced with an uncertain future, many of Hong Kong's residents will be forced to look elsewhere for assurance. At such a time their hearts may be open to the Gospel. Second, the Hong Kong church, which heretofore has not been particularly evangelistic, now has channeled more funds into training and evangelism. Finally, the realities of the approaching transition have fostered a greater sense of unity in the

Hong Kong church.

This sense of unity appeared as early as 1984 when, prior to the signing of the Draft Agreement, some 3,000 Hong Kong Christians packed a church to hear the contents of a statement written by 80 representatives of a variety of Hong Kong's 400 Protestant churches. The statement declared Protestants' desire for unity and renewal, for faithfulness to Christ, and a determination to resist compromise.

Certainly Christians all over the world need to intercede for Hong Kong. Not only does Hong Kong face an uncertain future but is a religious melting pot of almost all Asia's major religions. Even these religions, however, play a secondary role to the religion of materialism. Christians should pray for great spiritual breakthroughs in the next decade as well as for unity, fervency, and renewal within the Hong Kong church.

The Philippines

On the night of February 7,1986, the world rejoiced with Corazon Aquino as she stood, radiant in her symbolic yellow dress, waving the victory sign. The housewife, spouse of a slain political hero, arrived on a wave of good wishes and a ground swell of popular support. "People power" overthrew the corrupt regime of Ferdinand Marcos and announced to the world that the Philippines was choosing democracy. With surprising speed, the Philippine president of twenty-one years was whisked out of the country and the nation placed in the untried hands of a fifty-two-year-old woman.

In its long history, the Philippines has undergone three drastic changes of course. In 1521, during the Age of Exploration, Ferdinand Magellan claimed the islands for Spain. For the next 350 years, the Spanish influence in the Philippines left a permanent imprint upon the nation, most notably in the prominence of the Roman Catholic church. Spanish rule continued until 1898 when, as part of the spoils of victory in the Spanish-American War, the United States took possession of the Philippines.

From 1898 to 1946, the United States put a democratic face on the Philippines, but the oligarchic structure which had developed during Spanish rule remained. Land ownership continued in the hands of a limited number of powerful families. However, with a high priority given to education, literacy rates were boosted even though social and economic reforms lagged behind.

On July 4, 1946, the Philippines became an independent nation born in the ashes of the victory of World War II. The course of Philippine affairs after independence moved toward economic nationalism and away from dependence upon the United States. However, corruption, bribery, tax evasion, and the concentration of power in the hands of a few remained persistent problems.

Finally, in 1965, Ferdinand Marcos was elected president in what appeared to be a popular choice. The inadequacies of his later years in power should not obscure the fact that he was effective during his first few years in office. Re-elected in 1969, Marcos presided over a successful implementation of the Green Revolution in the 1960's which made the Philippines a bright hope in Asia's future. Some beginning steps were taken toward land redistribution but these failed to bring about a wider dispersion of wealth.

In the late 1960's, a gradual change occurred in Marcos' policies. His close relationship with the United States and his anti-communist stance brought the rewards of American foreign aid and investment. Marcos engaged in "crony capitalism" whereby his friends and supporters were awarded lucrative contracts for everything from sugar mills to luxury hotels. Social unrest in the early 1970's reflected the discontent of a nation in which the gap between the rich and poor grew wider each year.

In order to quell the demonstrations and unrest, Marcos imposed martial law in 1972. An amendment to a new constitution allowed Marcos to use emergency power which, in effect, gave Marcos dictatorial rather than presidential powers. Marcos' serious illness and obvious physical deterioration further complicated the political situation. Meanwhile the United States found itself in an increasingly delicate position. The need to maintain a strategic military presence at Clark Air Base and Subic Naval Base meant the embarrassment of supporting a Philippine president whose base of popular support was rapidly disintegrating.

Among Marcos' most vocal critics was a member of the legislature, Benigno Aquino. Because of his anti-government position, Aquino spent seven and a half years as a political prisoner, was put on trial, and sentenced to death for sedition. However, worldwide protests saved Aquino from execution and, in 1980, he was allowed to go to the United States for heart surgery.

The turning point in the course of events occurred on August 21, 1983 when, while attempting a return to Manila, Aquino was assassinated at the Manila airport. Filipinos responded in a highly emotional mixture of national grief and outrage while world opinion turned against Marcos. Few doubted that Marcos was somehow linked with the assassination.

What followed made matters worse. Censorship of the press and abuses of human rights led to more demonstrations and unrest. So-called "salvaging operations" by government soldiers to eliminate opposition were carried out under the guise of anti-communism. Meanwhile, the economy stagnated and foreign investment dwindled as other nations lost confidence in the Marcos government.

Finally, two major elements of Philippine society turned against Marcos: the middle class and the Roman Catholic church. Both of these conservative groups were incensed at Marcos' blatant corruption and his disregard for basic human rights. The U.S. pressed Marcos to call an election which was finally set for February of 1986.

The entry of Corazon Aquino into the electoral process came only with reluctance on her part and only after a realization that, as Benigno Aquino's widow, she possessed the popular appeal and rallying power to unite the opposition. The election was not without irregularities on both sides, but Mrs. Aquino emerged as a clear winner. When Marcos claimed victory, the army, inspired by General Fidel Ramos, rebelled and backed Aquino. By February 26, Ferdinand and Imelda Marcos fled to Hawaii, having looted the country of the incredible sum of betweeen five and ten billion dollars.

During Mrs. Aquino's first year in office, the honeymoon period, the government reeled from crisis to crisis. The nation discovered that it is easier to carry out a revolution than to establish a stable government. Whereas the Philippines had once been a measure of the success of the Green Revolution, now the most pressing problems were economic ones. In 1986, the nation carried a $27 billion foreign debt, per capita income was at an abysmal $600, and the nation actually suffered a negative economic growth rate of 3.5 per cent. At least 50 per cent of the nation's 21,000,000 workers were unemployed part of the year.

Among the steps the new president took were those to convince foreign creditors to grant the Philippines time and to increase foreign aid as well as foreign investment. By the end of 1987, the country's expected economic growth rate rose to an optimistic five per cent. Among other accomplishments of the first year was the adoption of a new consitution which provides a one-time-only presidential term of six years, a 24 member senate and a 250 member house of representatives. The national vote on both the new constitution and for the new legislative members were interpreted as continuing endorsements of Mrs. Aquino's popularity.

But the Philippines remains a beleagured nation with an uncertain future. Corruption in government remains an entrenched problem. Land reform still presents one of the most difficult of issues to resolve. At present, some 20 per cent of Filipinos own 80 per cent of the land. Much of President Aquino's support comes from the middle class, many of whom own medium-sized farms. Moreover, a decided preponderance of the members of the Philippine Congress are large landowners.

However, two major questions persist: First, how would landowners be compensated, and second, would land redistribution necessarily raise the level of productivity of the soil? One proposal would compensate landowners with some of the billions of dollars taken by Marcos and which the nation hopes to recover through legal means. The recovered money would also be used to educate newly landed farmers in the techniques of modern land management.

Unquestionably, the communist insurgency presents the Aquino government with its greatest and most dangerous challenge, not only because of its military presence but also because it is closely linked to poverty and social injustice. The communist military front, the New People's Army (N.P.A.) has established a presence in approximately 20 per cent of the rural area and claims to have 24,000 guerilla fighters. Unfortunately an attempted cease-fire in early 1987 ended in failure.

Consequently, citizens have formed vigilante groups, the best known of which is the Alsa Masa. Both popular and effective, the Alsa Masa has succeeded in driving back N.P.A. forces on the island of Mindanao. But violence, a traditional factor throughout most of the Philippines' history, increases as citizens take the law into their own hands.

The credibility of the Aquino government has been placed on the line by the ways in which the insurgency is dealt with and by the ways promises of reform are implemented. Evidence of the unstable political climate can be seen in the five coup attempts since the Aquino government came to power. Loyalty of the army to Mrs. Aquino remains a key factor in the survival of the struggling democracy.

When Christians view the current situation in the Philippines from a spiritual perspective, a different picture comes into focus. Benigno Aquino testified to a personal, born-again Christian experience while he was in jail. His wife Corazon, a devout believer, has attributed her election to a miracle from God. In the days just before the 1986 election, radio broadcasters and religious leaders called upon the nation to fast and pray. News reports from Manila showed courageous nuns boldly placing themselves in front of government soldiers. Indeed, many have suggested that the revolution was not just the result of "people power," but also of "prayer power."

While this is a time of great uncertainty in the Philippines, it is also a time of great opportunity. The whole Gospel for the whole man presents a greater appeal than ever before. From all walks of life, throughout the nation, Filipinos are responding to the Gospel in large numbers. Widespread Christian activity is conducted openly. The potential exists for Christians to truly and compassionately put the Gospel into action by coming to the aid of the great majority of Filipinos who live in impoverished circumstances.

Christians all over the world need to intercede in prayer on behalf of the Philippines. First, Christians ought to pray for Mrs. Aquino's personal safety and continued Christian commitment. Second, they should pray for stability, peace, and the success of a democratic government. If the Aquino government were to be toppled, a nationwide debacle would almost certainly ensue in which no one would be a winner. Prayer should be made for the unity and common purpose of Christians of all denominations. In a united, concerted effort the spiritual, political, and economic reconstruction of the nation can take place.

Furthermore, as great numbers of Filipinos respond to the Gospel, Christians need to pray for a greater number of people who are able to disciple and teach new believers. Both pastoral and lay workers are desperately needed. Finally, but by no means of lesser importance, world Christians need to pray for the personal safety of pastors, missionaries, and other Christian workers. In 1986 alone,

N.P.A. rebels killed 38 pastors and other Christian workers. No one can accurately predict the future of the Aquino government or of the Philippines. Thus a sense of urgency exists to take advantage of all present opportunities to share the good news of Jesus Christ in the Philippines.

India

Indian scholars, half humorously and half seriously, say: "When you have been in India for two weeks, you think you can write a book; when you have been in India for two months, you may be able to write a paper; when you have been in India for two years, you cannot write anything at all." The scholars are right. India defies attempts at definition and classification. No simple answers exist for the questions which India poses.

Upon first encounter, India bombards the senses. A whiff of sandalwood, the unnending cackle of thousands of blackbirds, the fiery first taste of curry, the graceful folds of a colorful sari—all form lingering impressions. With its diversity of religions, languages, traditions, and geography, no place in the world quite compares with India. But beneath its captivating, sometimes seductive qualities, lie enormous problems which threaten to splinter the great, proud nation, home of the world's largest democracy. That India exists at all must be considered a marvel.

Since India's independence in 1947, leadership of the nation has rested in the hands of one political family. India's prime ministership began with Jawaharlal Nehru, was passed to his daughter Indira Gandhi, and is now in the hands of Indira's son, Rajiv Gandhi. Indira Gandhi, who first became prime minister in 1966, seemed to be the very embodiment of India. Indians often said, "India is Indira and Indira is India." Even in mud-walled school houses in the remotest of villages, one could find photographs of Mrs. Gandhi. Although her policies were sometimes heavy-handed, no one else appeared to possess Mrs. Gandhi's capacity to provide leadership for India.

Then, on October 31, 1984, the world was stunned to hear of Indira Gandhi's assassination. Her death at the hands of her trusted Sikh bodyguards indicated the intensity of Sikh separatist aspirations. The prime ministership passed into the inexperienced hands of her son, Rajiv, whose political career consisted of a mere three years. At the age of forty and with no record of corruption, Rajiv was greeted with enthusiasm by a nation yearning for improved economic conditions and an efficient government.

By 1986, Gandhi's honeymoon period ended. Disenchantment with Gandhi's policies of conciliation and his failure to take a firm stand against government corruption have led to electoral losses for the traditionally strong Congress (I) Party, the party of Gandhi. Communist governments prevail in the influential states of West Bengal and Kerala.

Despite the enormous poverty of India and the declining popularity of the prime minister, India has actually made considerable economic progress in the 1980's. The nation whose name once was almost synonymous with the words hunger and starvation now not only produces a grain surplus, but actually exports wheat—the results of a successful Green Revolution. Nevertheless, economic growth is uneven in the huge subcontinent and depends on the uncertainties of the monsoon cycle. Average per capita income is still very low at $250 per year. Huge disparities exist; India has the technology to successfully launch a space satellite, yet in thousands of villages, the bullock cart continues to be the primary means of transportation.

But India's most volatile problems are ethnic and religious. Sikhs in the agriculturally rich northwest state of Punjab desire to break away and form their own nation of Khalistan. Although Sikhs represent a syncretic, monotheistic, religion for only two per cent of India's population, many of their numbers occupy positions of influence, particularly in the military. Rajiv Gandhi's attempts at reconciliation with the Sikhs have broken down and a solution appears a long way off. Meanwhile Sikh terrorist strikes on buses, airplanes, and in city streets continue.

The Indo-Pakistani border dispute continues to be one of the most dangerous flashpoints in the world. The issue, begun at partition in 1947, is complicated by the potential for the use of nuclear weapons. India has exploded a nuclear device but claims not to have a nuclear arsenal. Pakistan has not yet tested a nuclear weapon but possesses the necessary enriched uranium to do so. Settlement of the dispute has been further delayed by India's belief that Pakistan incites the Sikhs in the Punjab. Consequently, both nations have amassed troops along the border.

In neighboring Sri Lanka, where minority Hindu Tamils seek a separate state from the majority Buddhist Sinhalese, India also has a great deal at stake. Tamils in southern India may revive their own move for autonomy. Consequently, separatist movements by Sikhs and Tamils in addition to similar aspirations by ethnic and religious groups in the Indian states of Kashmir and Assam present India with the potential for much unrest in the years ahead.

From a Christian perspective, however, India represents one of Asia's greatest missionary challenges. Not quite three per cent of India's huge population of 750 million are Christian. Many are nominal second and third generation Christians with little fervency or evangelistic spirit. Visa policies prohibit missionaries from entering the country except as tourists or for professional reasons. Expiring missionary visas are rarely renewed.

The growth of a Hindu reconversion movement has meant more intense harassment of Christians. The Hindu religious awakening varies from greater intellectual curiosity of Hindu sacred scriptures to the militant Arya Samaj intent upon eradicating any religion other than Hinduism. Hindus are adopting the very evangelistic strategies once identified solely with Christianity.

Anti-Christian marches, destruction of churches, and persecution of pastors has marked the Hindu renaissance. Many Christians are forbidden to buy in the markets, their crops are stolen or destroyed, their children prevented from attending schools, and their traditional village foundations cut off.

Not only do Christians face Hindu opposition, but they also face increasing Islamic antagonism. With the availability of funds from oil-rich Islamic nations, Muslims actively engage in proselytizing and construction of expensive mosques. In some cases, whole villages have converted to Islam, often in an attempt to escape low-caste affiliation.

Despite such strong hindrances, Christianity is making inroads. In northern India, the state of Nagaland is almost entirely evangelical Christian. Elsewhere, thousands of Indians have responded to the powerful movie "Jesus" when it is shown in villages. Mobile film teams are able to reach villages where most are illiterate and where no access to television exists.

However, Christian literature still is one of the most effective evangelistic tools in India. Because the government has undertaken a concerted effort to raise literacy standards, a growing reading audience eager to read anything free or inexpensive is being created. Communists have been only too happy to take advantage of India's reading audience. Thus Christian literature organizations are confronted with a formidable challenge.

Christians throughout the world need to intercede for India, a nation once referred to by the Indian writer V.S. Naipaul as "a wounded civilization." Christians need to pray for the unity, peace, and stability of India. A splintered, bleeding India would be an Asian tragedy of huge proportions. Christians should pray for the placement of committed Christians in influential positions where they may have a voice in determining India's future. World Christians need to intercede on behalf of Christians in India who are being persecuted and on behalf of missionaries who desire to remain in India but encounter visa difficulties.

Prayer should be offered not only for finances to help spread the Gospel, but also for creative strategies to reach every level of Indian society, particularly the highest Hindu caste, the Brahmins. Brahmins, who occupy positions of authority and influence, have traditionally viewed Christianity as a religion more appealing to Untouchables. India is not a closed mission field nor is it a nation whose people are hopelessly lost, but the next decades will be crucial for the fulfillment of the Great Commission in India as its population approaches the one billion mark.

Chapter Twelve

In Conclusion

When we "spy out" Asia, as the men of Israel spied out Canaan, we see a continent in transition. Winds of change are blowing across Asia, reaching as far as the village level. Where once the world looked to the West as the source of the wave of the future, today the world is looking Eastward, toward Asia, where nearly two-thirds of the people of the world make their home. Bursting with potential, Asia is now the focal point of intensive economic activity and its accompanying political and social changes.

Yet, as we have seen, much of Asia still lies within the context of the Third World. China and the nations of both Southeast Asia and South Asia remain predominantly rural and exist in a pattern in which the cycle of the seasons dominates human activity. However, the trend toward urbanization represents one of the major transitional factors of Asia. Nations which are predominantly rural today will have a very different configuration by the year 2010. For example, projections suggest that by the year 2010 some 56 per cent of Filipinos will live in urban areas as will 42 per cent of Indians. That means that adequate housing, jobs, and the provision of human services will become even greater challenges in the years ahead.

The tragedy of human underdevelopment continues as a major problem in Asia. Malnutrition, disease, contaminated water, and illiteracy persist in the same Asia that possesses nuclear technology, that produces every conceivable electronic gadget, and that floods the world with its manufactured goods. Glaring contrasts greet the eye. In a matter of a few hours, a traveler can be whisked from Singapore's clean, flower-lined avenues to Calcutta's noisy, teaming streets, home of the homeless.

Millions of women still remain subjugated, ill-treated, and illiterate in the same Asia in which three nations (India, Sri Lanka, and the Philippines) have elected female heads of state. In both urban and rural areas, hundreds of thousands of mistreated children present a picture of tragedy and human exploitation as their backs become broken in fields and factories or their bodies sold into prostitution.

In a unique stance, Asia presently plants one foot in the past and one foot in the future. Traditionalism vs. modernization—the clash continues at every level and in every nation. Like the rest of the world, Asia has been incorporated into the global village. The traditional foundations that gave Asian societies stability and security now are being shaken.

The expectation explosion, fostered by modernization and the extension of the global village, has planted seeds of materialism, disillusionment, rebelliousness, and restlessness, particularly among youth. Evidence of these transitional characteristics can best be seen in nations like Japan and the newly industrialized countries such as South Korea, Taiwan, Singapore, and Hong Kong. But other nations of Asia are just one step behind. Already, the same harvest from the expectation explosion can be seen in Bombay, Shanghai, Bangkok, Jakarta, Manila, and other large cities of Asia.

However, as the weight of present problems and the uncertainties of the future press in upon Asia, greater opportunities than ever before present themselves for a compassionate Christian response. Biblical Christianity offers a whole Gospel for the whole man which, when truly implemented in deed as well as word, advances the hope of permanent change. Such Asian areas as Nagaland and Kerala in India, the Karen tribal region in Burma, and West Timor in Indonesia offer evidence of Christian change.

But the very geography of Asia looms as a deterrent in the task of fullfilling the Great Commission. While the diversity of Asian geography can be viewed as evidence of the magnificent greatness of the Creator, isolation and fragmentation present challenges for mission strategy. From the soaring Himalayas cutting Asia in half to the thousands of islands of Southeast Asia, the great continent forms a complex geographic pattern.

Asia's history reaches farther back into antiquity than the Western mind can comprehend. Wave upon wave of momentous events swept the continent, from invasions to civil wars to the rise and fall of dynsties. One thing is certain: the redemptive plan of a sovereign God was, and is, being carried out. Throughout history, God has moved decisively to intervene in the affairs of men. In His timing, God arranged for the Apostle Thomas to bring the good news of who Jesus is to the Indian subcontinent.

Many years later, Queen Elizabeth I could not have imagined that on the eve of 1600 when she created the British East India Co., she was inaugurating an era that would bring far more than material trade to Asia. Where traders went, missionaries soon followed. In obscure places, in countless unrecognized ways, these courageous Christian pioneers sewed seeds from which modern missionaries are reaping a harvest.

In another example of God's sovereignty, no one could have foreseen that when the evils of opium erupted into war between China and Great Britain, God would turn the resulting unequal treaty system into a vehicle for His redemptive plan for China. As treaty ports in China were opened to traders, so they were also opened to missionaries, who soon gained access to the interior.

In more recent Chinese history, who could have predicted in 1949, when the communists came to power, that forty years later China would have one of the largest, most fervent churches in the world? Even the communists became the instruments of a sovereign God to build roads, facilitate the availability of radio and television, and reduce languages to one major language—all of which have aided the spread of the Gospel in China.

With these lessons of the past in mind, Christians can justifiably look at Asia today and speculate about the ways in which God is intervening in the affairs of men. Momentous events are taking place with increasing speed. Where once changes in Asia took place over decades or even centuries, today the pace of change is so rapid that the many new events are difficult to absorb.

Overnight a Christian woman was placed in power in the Philippines. The entire direction of Chinese affairs has turned in less than a decade. The shocking pull of a trigger altered India's leadership dramatically. In little more than two decades, South Korea jumped from being an impoverished nation devastated by war to becoming a newly industrialized Asian power. With the signature on an agreement, Hong Kong's entire future was drastically reshaped.

However, one area of Asian life remains rooted in the past and continues to hold a persistent and pervasive influence: that of Asian religions. Hinduism, Buddhism, Islam, Confucianism, Taoism, Shintoism—all either are maintaining strength or are experiencing increased influence. The cultural identity of many Asian nations, such as India, Thailand, and Pakistan, remains inseparable from their religions. In East Asia, Confucian, Taoist, and Buddhist values subtly perservere even in the midst of high technology.

A Hindu reconversion movement in India is reminiscent of the Hindu renaissance of the eighteenth century. With fiery conviction backed by the power of petrodollars, Muslims aggressively proselytize throughout Asia. Along with textiles, autos, and electronic devices, Asia exports its mantras, its gurus, and its sacred scriptures to eager New

Agers in the West.

Nevertheless, promising Christian developments appear in many nations of Asia. The church is growing three times as fast as the population in Asia. The strongly evangelistic church of South Korea and the fervent, suffering church of China have altered the religious configuration of East Asia. Elsewhere, positive response to the Gospel and an increased pace of church planting in such nations as the Philippines, Thailand, India, and Indonesia indicate a developing Christian momentum in Asia.

However, in fourteen nations of Asia, fewer than one per cent of the population is Christian. Nations such as North Korea, Laos, Vietnam, and Kampuchea are entirely closed to mission activity. In many other nations, including Nepal, Malaysia, and Pakistan, Christian missionary activity is severely restricted.

Still others, most notably India, have added visa restrictions which further complicate missionary activity. In fact, in only nine Asian nations are Western missionaries allowed unrestricted access.

But the face of Asian missions is changing. Because so many nations are closing to Western missionaries, the day of the Western missionary playing the preeminent role in Asian missions is coming to an end. The Great Commission is not just a Western mandate, but a global mandate and will be carried out by an army of volunteers from all over the world. The future trend of Asian missions will thrust Asian missionaries into a dominant role as they evangelize other Asians.

Not only are Asian missionaries to be found in their own nations, but they will continue to be a growing factor in world missions. South Korea alone already has missionaries in 47 other countries. Projections suggest that by the year 2000, some 67,000 Asian missionaries will be actively engaged in sharing the Gospel worldwide. As the twentieth century enters its last decade, the greatest missionary thrust in history will combine missionaries from all nations, races, and cultures in a shared role for a common cause.

Certainly sheer numbers of missionaries are vital as are the release of finances and the development of appropriate mission strategies. But the single most crucial factor in the fulfillment of the Great Commission is prayer. When we pray, God acts. The matter is that simple—and that powerful. Prayer is that avenue whereby we bring God into a situation; therefore, prayer cannot be thought of as a last resort or even as a choice. Rather, prayer comprises the first step of all mission enterprises.

Whether or not the reader of this book ever sets foot on the Asian continent is secondary. Asia, and indeed the rest of the world, will be changed through the power generated in the intimacy and privacy of the prayer closet. A Christian need go no further than his bended knee and bowed head to have a part in evangelizing Asia. Every Christian, wherever he is or whatever his circumstances, can intercede for nations and thus play a crucial part in changing the world.

Christ told His disciples in Matthew 11:12 that "From the days of John the Baptist until now, the kingdom of heaven has been forcefully advancing, and forceful men lay hold of it." Christ's kingdom here on earth will be advanced by committed, courageous Christians willing to wage spiritual warfare. The victories come in that place of prayer. Satan is a defeated foe and his spiritual strongholds in Asia will be brought down, not by concentrating on the power of the enemy, but by standing fast in the knowledge of what God can do when His people call upon Him in prayer.

Because God's plan for all mankind is a redemptive plan, Asia is included. This does not mean, however, that every Asian will become a Christian. Sadly, in Asia as elsewhere, many will reject Christ, but Christians have a responsibility to see to it that all Asians are offered the opportunity to respond to the Gospel.

Today, a sense of urgency charges all evangelistic endeavors. The fulfillment of Biblical prophecy in our own time points to the return soon of the Bridegroom for His Bride, the Church. What, then, is our responsibility as Christians? First, to make certain that our own lives are characterized by the fear of the Lord and the call to holiness and godliness. Second, to pray, not only for nations across the world, but also for our own families and our own nations. We can only be as effective as individuals in prayer according to the degree that our hearts are open before the Lord.

Third, we have a responsibility to allow ourselves to be available to our Commander-in-Chief to be sent to the mission field if He so desires. Numerous opportunities, both long-term and short-term, await in a variety of mission organizations. Professionals such as doctors, nurses, teachers, and agricultural experts are allowed access to areas where missionaries are restricted. Doctors may volunteer for two week projects or teachers may teach English as a second language. Mission opportunities can be found for a diversity of skills such as computer experts, engineers, hotel managers, and performing artists. Our fourth responsibility is to give generously of our resources in whatever way possible to support mission efforts.

Finally, whatever God's plans for Asia, they are precisely that—His plans. He alone holds the divine blueprint. While He uses people to accomplish His sovereign will, the glory of accomplishment is all His.

"All the nations you have made will come and worship before you, O Lord; they will bring glory to your name." Psalm 86:9.

Suggestions for Further Reading

Anderson, Sir Norman. *Christianity and World Religions.* Downers Grove: Intervarsity Press, 1984.

Gibson, Noel and Phyl. *Evicting Demonic Squatters and Breaking Bondages.* Drummoyne, N.S.W., Australia: Freedom in Christ Ministries, 1987.

Groothius, Douglas R. *Unmasking the New Age.* Downers Grove: Intervarsity Press, 1986.

Johnstone, Patrick. *Operation World.* Fort Washington, Pennsylvania: WEC International, 1986.

Lawrence, Carl. The *Church in China.* Minneapolis: Bethany House Publishers, 1985.

Pollock, J.C. *Hudson Taylor and Maria, Pioneers in China.* Grand Rapids: Zondervan Publishing House, 1976.

Richardson, Don. *Eternity in Their Hearts.* Ventura, California: Regal Books, 1984.

Tooley, Ross. *We Cannot But Tell.* Seattle: Frontline Publications, 1988.

Tucker, Ruth. *From Jerusalem to Irian Jaya.* Grand Rapids: The Zondervan Corporation, 1983.

Winter, Ralph D. and Steven C. Hawthorne, eds. *Perspectives on the World Christian Movement.* Pasadena: William Carey, 1982.

You may purchase these books from the following distributors in your country:

USA
Frontline Communications
P.O. Box 55787
Seattle, Washington 98155
(206) 771-1153

AUSTRALIA
Christian Marketing
P.O. Box 154
North Geelong, VIC 3215
(052) 78-6100

CANADA
Scripture In Song
P.O. Box 550
Virgil, ONT LOS 1TO
(416) 468-4214

ENGLAND
Mannafest Books
Holmsted Manor, Staplefield Rd.
Cuckfield, W. Sussex RH17 5JF
(0444) 440229

GERMANY
Youth With A Mission
Military Ministries
Mozart Str. 15
8901 Augsburg — Stadtbergen
(0821) 522659

HOLLAND
Pelgrim Intl. Boekenckm
Rijnstraat 12
6811 EV Arnheim

HONG KONG
Jensco, Ltd.
10 Borrett Road
(5) 246-057

NEW ZEALAND
Concord Distributors, Ltd.
Private Bag
Havelock North
(070) 778-161

SOUTH AFRICA
Mannafest Media
Private Bag X0018
Delmas 2210
(0157) 3317

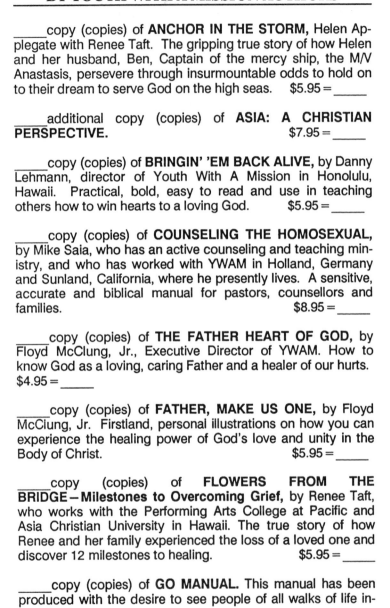

OTHER LIFE-CHANGING BOOKS
BY YOUTH WITH A MISSION AUTHORS

_____copy (copies) of **ANCHOR IN THE STORM,** Helen Applegate with Renee Taft. The gripping true story of how Helen and her husband, Ben, Captain of the mercy ship, the M/V Anastasis, persevere through insurmountable odds to hold on to their dream to serve God on the high seas. $5.95 = _____

_____additional copy (copies) of **ASIA: A CHRISTIAN PERSPECTIVE.** $7.95 = _____

_____copy (copies) of **BRINGIN' 'EM BACK ALIVE,** by Danny Lehmann, director of Youth With A Mission in Honolulu, Hawaii. Practical, bold, easy to read and use in teaching others how to win hearts to a loving God. $5.95 = _____

_____copy (copies) of **COUNSELING THE HOMOSEXUAL,** by Mike Saia, who has an active counseling and teaching ministry, and who has worked with YWAM in Holland, Germany and Sunland, California, where he presently lives. A sensitive, accurate and biblical manual for pastors, counsellors and families. $8.95 = _____

_____copy (copies) of **THE FATHER HEART OF GOD,** by Floyd McClung, Jr., Executive Director of YWAM. How to know God as a loving, caring Father and a healer of our hurts. $4.95 = _____

_____copy (copies) of **FATHER, MAKE US ONE,** by Floyd McClung, Jr. Firstland, personal illustrations on how you can experience the healing power of God's love and unity in the Body of Christ. $5.95 = _____

_____copy (copies) of **FLOWERS FROM THE BRIDGE — Milestones to Overcoming Grief,** by Renee Taft, who works with the Performing Arts College at Pacific and Asia Christian University in Hawaii. The true story of how Renee and her family experienced the loss of a loved one and discover 12 milestones to healing. $5.95 = _____

_____copy (copies) of **GO MANUAL.** This manual has been produced with the desire to see people of all walks of life involved in missions. It lists over 2,500 short- and long-term opportunities and further training possibilities in over 60 countries, involving more than 140 YWAM locations.

$1.95 = _____

_____copy (copies) of **INTIMATE FRIENDSHIP WITH GOD,** by Joy Dawson, a dynamic communicator and teacher. Keys to knowing, obeying and loving God. $5.95 = _____

_____copy (copies) of **IS THAT REALLY YOU, GOD?,** Loren Cunningham with Janice Rogers. The exciting beginnings of Youth With A Mission as Loren Cunningham discovers keys to hearing God's voice. $5.95 = _____

_____copy (copies) of **LIVING ON THE DEVIL'S DOORSTEP,** by Floyd McClung, Jr. Join Floyd and his wife, Sally, as they live first in a hippie hotel in Afghanistan and then next door to prostitutes, pimps, drug dealers and homosexuals in Amsterdam. $8.95 = _____

_____copy (copies) of **PERSONAL PRAYER DIARY — DAILY PLANNER.** A quiet time journal using a week-at-a-glance format that allows a daily record of your times alone with God. Ideal for home, office or as a gift. Great for busy people!

$9.95 = _____

_____copy (copies) of **WE CANNOT BUT TELL,** by Ross Tooley, a pioneering missionary with extensive experience in frontline, eye-to-eye evangelism; leader of the YWAM work in the Philippines for 13 years. A manual on how to prepare, present, and preserve the results in personal evangelism.

$5.95 = _____

_____copy (copies) of **WINNING, GOD'S WAY,** Loren Cunningham with Janice Rogers. How you can experience a victorious Christian life as you discover new freedom, joy and power through living God's way. $5.95 = _____

_____copy (copies) 6-cassette album of **ARE THERE ANSWERS...To the Difficult Questions People Ask?** by Loren Cunningham.   1)Can You Prove There Is a God? 2)What Kind of Personality Does God Have?   3)Why the

Cross? 4)Creating With God 5)Why War? 6)How Can a God of Love Send a Man To Hell? $24.95 = _____

_____copy (copies) 6-cassette album of **LET'S TURN THE WORLD AROUND**, by Loren Cunningham. 1)Let's Turn the World Around 2) Let's Go Barefoot, 3)Conditions For Knowing God's Voice, 4)Creating With God, 5)Go Means a Change of Location, 6) Releasing the Power of the Spirit. $24.95 = _____

$2.00 postage for 1-2 books/cassette albums plus .25 for each additional book.

Quantity Discount

4-9 items	**10% discount**
10-24 items	**20% discount**
25 items or more	**42% discount**

For Visa/MasterCard orders only call 1-800-922-2143

Number_____Expiration Date___ ___

Signature_____

ORDER NOW!

Send your order and payment to:

Frontline Communications — YWAM
P.O. Box 55787
Seattle, Washington 98155
(206) 771-1153

_____ Enclosed is $_____

Name

_____

Address

_____

City and State   Zip Code

_____(Check) For additional information on Youth With A Mission and a book/cassette catalogue.